The Employable Sociologist

Martha A. Martinez

The Employable Sociologist
A Guide for Undergraduates

palgrave
macmillan

Martha A. Martinez
Sociology
DePaul University
Chicago, IL, USA

ISBN 978-3-031-41322-3   ISBN 978-3-031-41323-0 (eBook)
https://doi.org/10.1007/978-3-031-41323-0

© The Editor(s) (if applicable) and The Author(s), under exclusive licence to Springer Nature Switzerland AG 2023

This work is subject to copyright. All rights are solely and exclusively licensed by the Publisher, whether the whole or part of the material is concerned, specifically the rights of translation, reprinting, reuse of illustrations, recitation, broadcasting, reproduction on microfilms or in any other physical way, and transmission or information storage and retrieval, electronic adaptation, computer software, or by similar or dissimilar methodology now known or hereafter developed.

The use of general descriptive names, registered names, trademarks, service marks, etc. in this publication does not imply, even in the absence of a specific statement, that such names are exempt from the relevant protective laws and regulations and therefore free for general use.

The publisher, the authors, and the editors are safe to assume that the advice and information in this book are believed to be true and accurate at the date of publication. Neither the publisher nor the authors or the editors give a warranty, expressed or implied, with respect to the material contained herein or for any errors or omissions that may have been made. The publisher remains neutral with regard to jurisdictional claims in published maps and institutional affiliations.

Cover illustration: © Alex Linch shutterstock.com

This Palgrave Macmillan imprint is published by the registered company Springer Nature Switzerland AG.
The registered company address is: Gewerbestrasse 11, 6330 Cham, Switzerland

Paper in this product is recyclable.

Acknowledgments

Books are like children; raising them takes a village. While I want to believe that this book provides innovative tools, I am building it from the foundation created by previous sociologists, among them Mary Senter, who so graciously reviewed my book proposal and supported the project at different stages. I need to thank Jessica Bishop-Royse for her early feedback and support; without her and her righteous anger in support of Sociology students, this book would not have moved from its early stages. I am eternally grateful to all my former students for being the inspiration and source for the topics and examples in this book. Nicole Bennett, Daniela Saavedra, and Gina Foster deserve a special mention for generously donating their resumes in progress. My sincere thanks to Ellie Santonato for making sure that I represented the knowledge of career centers faithfully. And given my copy-editing limitations, I have to give a shout out to Linda Levendusky for making sure that I do not use five words when three will suffice.

Contents

Part I The Sociological Identity   1

1 Introduction 3
2 A Sociological Professional Identity 17
3 The Values of Sociology 35
4 Community Building for Sociologists 49
5 Networking for Sociologists 65

Part II Transferable Skills   79

6 A Sociological View of the Resume 81
7 Skills in the Sociology Major 99
8 The Language of Business 117
9 An Identity-Based Job Search 135

Part III Career Management   153

10 A Sociological View of Managerial Behavior 155
11 The Selection Process 169
12 From Jobs to Careers 187

Index 201

List of Figures

Fig. 4.1	Professional reflective journal	60
Fig. 6.1	Sample Resume Nicole Bennett	87
Fig. 6.2	Sample Resume Gina Foster	92
Fig. 6.3	Sample Resume Daniela Saavedra	94
Fig. 9.1	Global Asset Map	137
Fig. 9.2	Cover Letter Template	146
Fig. 9.3	Job Posting Example	147
Fig. 9.4	Cover Letter Example	148

List of Tables

Table 4.1	Nonprofit trade publications	59
Table 4.2	Social media publications	59
Table 5.1	Sample questions for informational interview	77
Table 6.1	List of resume conventions	90
Table 7.1	Software Commonly Used by Sociology Students	101
Table 7.2	Research Skills/Methodologies	102
Table 7.3	Interagency Language Roundtable (ILR) Scale	103
Table 7.4	NACE Competencies and their Sociological Equivalents	105
Table 7.5	Socioemotional Skills	110
Table 8.1	Revised Bloom's Taxonomy of Action Words	130
Table 9.1	Potential Keywords for Job Searches	142

Part I
The Sociological Identity

Introduction 1

Twenty-five years ago when I graduated with a BA in Communication in Mexico, I felt lost and hopeless. Most of my formative years had coincided with the "lost decade" of Latin America, a time of persistent economic crisis marked by hyperinflation, high unemployment, and overall pessimism about the future. By the time I finished my studies in December 1994, Mexico was experiencing one of the biggest financial crises in its history, popularly called the December Error. With unemployment levels twice that of the general population, we recent college graduates could not catch a break.

My problems went beyond the already significant economic crisis and a depressed labor market. As a Communication major, I knew (or thought) I had skills; I just did not know to transfer them into a successful professional life. I was a first-generation college woman with no money and no connections. I remember telling a friend I wish I had been taught how to look for a job. This was the beginning of the Internet era and the debut of Gopher, the first web browser, and Yahoo, the first search tool. However, public information about jobs was still limited to newspaper ads. I eventually found jobs, but once I had them I did not know how to use them to develop a career. I wrote for employee magazines, I advised Business students in my alma mater, and I became a kick-ass Spanish-English translator that almost got me hired by NXIVM, the now infamous professional development/sex cult company. Eventually, I decided to immigrate to the United States and follow an academic path. The clarity of academia's step-by-step career guidelines and expected rites of passages appealed to me. I also decided to leave the communications field and get a degree in Economic Sociology. I wanted to know why I could not make it work in the "real world" and how others overcame obstacles to find social mobility and success. My focus turned to the study of networks, organizational dynamics, entrepreneurship, and markets.

Decades later, something about the universality of human experience still applies. My current and former Sociology students tell me they feel very much the way I did almost 30 years ago. The majors have changed and so have the surrounding technological and economic conditions. But the anxiety, confusion, and sense of crisis remain the same. Popular imagination holds that good jobs and opportunities were abundant not so long ago in the United States. Personally, I doubt that well-paid jobs ever just magically landed in people's laps (or laptops today). Right now, many young people, including Sociology undergraduate students, do have reason to worry about their prospects. You may personally share many of these worries yourself. Education gets increasingly more expensive and the likelihood of landing good-paying jobs less certain. Your parents may be warning you that Sociology is not a "practical" major. Your professors may be offering you inadequate support and career advice. You may even hear that you are wasting your time pursuing a college degree. These complaints fall into three issue areas: cost versus benefit, the purpose of the university, and the potential use of Sociology in the workplace. This book will explore these problems and offer you an expanded concept of your own employability to help you and other Sociology majors manage and overcome these current and perennial problems.

The Neoliberal Education and the Problem of Cost

The idea that higher education should translate into high-paying jobs dominates neoliberal narratives. Neoliberalism has been the main ideological theory for understanding the relationships between institutions and society during the last 30 years. Neoliberalism regards education as an individual investment and free economic markets as the best mechanisms for providing the best education from the perspective of both individuals and society. Under this theory, individuals can achieve their own personal goals by choosing (and paying for) a variety of educational choices. The aggregate effect of these choices provides society with the optimal quantity and quality of education. Education providers are motivated to offer the best education possible to attract the most or the most sought-after consumers (students).

As a sociologist, I have three arguments to challenge the neoliberal view of education. First, education is an imperfect market. Individuals cannot really evaluate the quality of an education without going through the process itself, at which point they have already paid for it. Nor is much information available for employers to evaluate or compare the potential value of a worker educated from one university versus another. Therefore, both applicants and employers use reputation or personal connections as the basis to judge the "education." Second, individuals and society also receive benefits from education that go beyond the sales market; there are benefits to education that are literally "priceless." The third and most relevant criticism of neoliberal educational policies concerns the effects of government-sponsored credit. In practice, this philosophy endorsing "choice" has resulted in transferring the bulk of the cost of education to students and their families, while reducing the amount of "social investment" in education through reduced public budgets. This transformation has relied on the use of government-sponsored loans that are readily available to most US citizens. Students can fund 100% of their educational expenses through loans. The availability of easy money has created incentives for tuition price hikes and disincentives for cost savings by universities. Even before the Great Recession forced many public universities to increase their tuition rates, the costs of higher education were shifting from the government to individual students and their families. Before neoliberalism became predominant, higher education was considered affordable. In 1980, annual tuition and fees at a private, four-year university averaged $10,546 compared to $2413 at a four-year public university (Hanson, 2022). By 2010, that cost had risen to $31,700 and $8500, respectively. The Great Recession continued the trend toward higher prices, with costs in 2020 averaging $37,600 for private, nonprofit universities and $9400 for public universities, respectively (NCES, 2022).[1] Not surprisingly, education has been one of the few sectors in which inflation has remained high over the whole 30-year course of controlled inflation created by neoliberalism.

The use of credit to fund education translates into debt. Student debt has become the second leading source of consumer indebtedness (mortgages are first), totaling an estimated $1.6 trillion in 2022. The type of borrowers and the size of debts vary widely, as do the methods for calculating those numbers. Since my purpose is to get a general sense of the size of the problem, I will use figures popularized by general media. *Forbes* calculates that students graduating with a degree from a public university in 2020 had an average debt of $30,030, compared to an average of $33,900 for graduates of nonprofit, private colleges and $43,900 for those graduating from for-profit colleges and universities (Friedman, 2021).

While educational costs have increased, the monetary "return on investment" of education has become more uncertain. A college degree produces higher earnings at all stages over the course of a lifetime compared to high school graduates. Those differences, however, appear to have become smaller than they used to be

---

[1] All tuition costs by year are expressed in 2021 dollars for more accurate comparison.

(Tamborini et al., 2015). Lifetime earnings associated with getting a college degree compared to only a high school degree vary significantly by major. In 2015, authors Kim, Tamborini, and Sakamoto matched the Survey of Income and Program Participation (SIPP) for 2004 and 2008 with data from the Detailed Earnings Record (DER) files at the Social Security Administration and found the gain in lifetime earnings attributable to a STEM BA compared to a high school diploma was $800,000. The earnings gain of a social sciences graduate (in this case including Psychology, History, and Communication) was only $374,000.[2] Problems associated with debt repayment are compounded by repayment schedules. Graduates must start paying off their loans early in their careers before they've realized the full financial benefits of a college education, which may leave them feeling cheated by their degrees. That does not mean that debt is not a real problem; it makes borrowers' first few years after graduation more difficult and delays life transitions like independent living (Houle & Warner, 2017), marriage (Addo et al., 2019), homeownership (Mezza et al., 2020), and savings accumulation (Elliott & Lewis, 2015). This burden is a direct result of neoliberal policies.

Average returns on income through education are real and significant, but they are not assured. Intra-occupational inequality, that is differences in earnings among individuals with the same occupation, have also increased in the twenty-first century (Kim & Sakamoto, 2008). Gender, race, geography, and many other social variables also can affect returns on education negatively. The effect of social background is particularly relevant for many Sociology students, who tend to come disproportionally from minority groups. According to the American Sociological Association, 70.4% of Sociology degrees awarded in 2017 were to females, 25.2% to Hispanics, and 18.4% to African Americans. Compare these numbers to the distributions for general BAs, with 57% granted to women, 13.5% to Latinos, and 10.5% to African Americans. The presence of minority students in Sociology is considerably higher than Business majors for example. For school year 2016–2017, only 10.3% of Business majors were African American, 11.4% Hispanic, and 48.3% female (NCES, 2016–2017). Although the American Sociological Association does not keep statistics on first-generation college Sociology majors, we know that for the general college population in the 2015–2016 academic year, 56% of students were the first members of their families to enter college (RTI, 2019). First-generation college status is associated with an absence of material and

---

[2] This figure illustrates past differences (by definition, lifetime earnings only count older individuals), and does not necessarily indicate the returns current students can expect to earn over their careers. However, such numbers provide a good gauge of the differences between majors.

cultural resources to utilize in transitioning from school to work and a negative effect on graduates' overall incomes. Given both increasingly higher costs of education and higher levels of income and wealth inequality brought about by neoliberalism, a BA degree may be insufficient for ensuring financially and personally satisfying careers.

The Problem of the University as an Institution

Society blames the high costs surrounding higher education not on neoliberal capitalism or government policies, but on universities and educational programs themselves. In the public imagination (including that of mass media), the institution of the university appears to be experiencing a crisis of resources and values. The university is often depicted as out of touch with the realities that our students, alumni, and society in general must face. We are seen as a poor fit to modern society and slow to adapt to the requirements of twenty-first-century capitalism. The reasons for this crisis are myriad, and many stem from the continuation of processes that have been going on for decades. That includes the popularization of online education, either out of personal choice or the necessities related to the COVID-19 pandemic; demographic changes that will shrink the number of college-age students over time; increased competition by a growing number of for-profit educational institutions; greater global competition for international students; and the stagnation of tenure-track positions amidst a growth in contract and part-time ones. Universities are being asked to justify their existence (and their costs) by parents, students, government, and society in general. Given that more students now must pay their own way, Sociology faculty should be able to offer clear "value" to them. But calculating "value" requires a definition of what exactly universities do or should do. Universities fulfill multiple and contradictory functions and serve multiple masters: they create, preserve, and diffuse knowledge; they both support and question the status quo, preserving useful traditions and promoting social progress; they contribute to the development of an educated and productive labor force; they educate individuals to be functional and responsible members of society, and they empower individuals to achieve their personal and professional goals. These functions and priorities are not distributed homogenously across universities or even inside universities; different departments and even different faculty within departments have their own theories about what the university should be and the right order of priorities.

These conflicts are not new. Since capitalism's advent as the predominant form of economic organization, academia has faced tensions between the goal of education as a mechanism for virtue or as a response to the practical needs of its consumers, and, therefore, capitalism. This tension has historically resulted in the evolution of the university as an institution and a creation of professional schools that align themselves with specific occupations and economic sectors (Stabile, 2007). The Social Sciences and the Humanities have continued with more or less traditional curriculums and programs based on the historical structure of their disciplines. While all university programs are criticized for being overly expensive, the "value" of the Social Sciences and the Humanities is questioned the most.

To me, the value of education goes beyond economic benefits. However, I can understand why students, parents, and society may worry about future income. Wage data supports the idea that certain majors provide higher "value," but offer a mixed picture concerning the value of the Social Sciences in the minds of employers. Consider comparative data for three fields that I think are more closely in competition with each other: Business, Social Sciences, and Humanities. According to the National Association of Colleges and Employers (NACE), in 2021 employers expected to pay Social Science graduates starting their careers an average salary of $59,919, Humanities graduates $59,500, and Business majors $58,869. However, there is a big gap between intent and actual wage offerings. The graduating class of 2021 ended up with a median starting salary of $60,966 for those in the Social Sciences, $60,534 for Business majors, and $47,554 for Humanities students. Sociology was near the lower end of the Social Sciences spectrum, with a median wage of $53,500, below Psychology ($58,840), Political Science ($57,500), and Economics ($65,000) (NACE, 2022). These numbers indicate relatively small differences in how employers value different majors in the abstract. In practice, however, recent graduates experience quite different outcomes in their job searches.

The Problem of the "Usefulness" of Sociology

Sociology faculty have little control over the cost or the economic benefits of education. They do, however, have some control over how they teach and practice Sociology. We professors should consider students' future careers in our teaching. Some of my colleagues may criticize me for framing the debate over the value of our discipline through capitalism. Fair point. Many academics understandably balk at the idea of reducing college education to a "value" proposition: an investment with a particular cost-benefit. This view argues that a preoccupation with questions like employability, social mobility, and lifetime earnings leads to treating higher education as a business, and the inevitable McDonalization of education (Roberts

& Donahue, 2000). Education becomes mechanical, uncritical, superficial, and narrow. It produces worker bees—individuals blindly following a system they neither question nor understand. From this perspective, a lack of ethical and moral values at the center of an education is the root cause of social problems like corruption, discrimination, and lack of empathy. It maintains that the pursuit of economic value compromises the development of desirable moral values as part of the educational experience.

Many Sociology students agree. If they wanted a more "practical" major, they would have selected it. Sociology students in general tend to choose their major out of a desire to use knowledge to improve the world and themselves. They want to study the systems that have impacted them personally so that they can help others navigate them. They would rather get paid less than be stuck in a soulless, higher-paying job. Like many of my students, you too may want to work for a nonprofit, serve a vulnerable population, and actively reform systems. Being a sociologist equates to being fair, empathetic, community-oriented, and interculturally fluent, among many other virtues.

A willingness to exchange money for job satisfaction is a personal choice. However, in talking about careers with my students I caution them to beware of the "system's" use of their good intentions to exploit and alienate them. I see that sometimes their job choices, or their procrastination in making them, are rooted in anxiety and confusion. These fears may stem from the causes that follow.

Skepticism from Family, Friends, and Potential Strangers to Sociology

One of my students provided a good example of hostility toward Sociology. She was standing outside a school building and because it was late she took a shared Uber to her apartment. Her companions, a very drunk couple, asked her what she studied. When she answered Sociology they exclaimed loudly, "What the F$#@ … is that?" Many parents and employers share this sentiment; they may just be a little more polite in expressing it. You may have had similar experiences. In current debates on the value of education, Sociology gets placed squarely in the company of the Humanities. Indeed, sociologists share many of the excellent skills of their English and Philosophy counterparts. But the core of our training in the use of the scientific method sets us apart from the Humanities. We obviously have an image problem since this difference is hardly ever recognized. Unless employers have some personal experience with Sociology, they really do not know the skills and expertise it demands. Your job as a sociologist is to help "sell" our discipline.

Lack of Confidence in One's Skills and Knowledge

This is the most common career development issue among Sociology students and the one that surprises me most. Students and alumni feel they have no skills to offer, particularly compared to other majors. I am happy to assure them that we have numerous advantages. We collect and analyze both quantitative and qualitative data. When it comes to data analysis, we are excellent at not just seeing numbers, but at knowing what they mean in relation to people's experiences. Our theories offer alternative views that both help define and explain issues. Our knowledge has been absorbed by many "practical" disciplines, including Human Resources, Management, and Economics. It saddens me to hear that our students may feel less qualified than other majors in any way.

Lack of Knowledge of Professional Options

This is a true weakness of the Sociology curriculum. Many faculty believe that career exploration should be independent of the classroom. Some of this avoidance comes from our lack of experience in traditional labor markets. Even as an expert in Economic Sociology, I have trouble keeping up with the constant transformations in work and occupations. You may encounter faculty who think everyone should get a PhD and enter academia. Many of your professors think the value of Sociology is self-apparent. Sociology is a wonderful discipline, one that provides skills applicable to a myriad of positions in almost any industry; our advantage is flexibility. Yet, the absence of standard career paths can have a paralyzing effect. Other Sociology faculty may see the need for career development assistance, but they consider that the responsibility of university career centers. In my experience, career centers can provide invaluable services, but they may not fully understand the scope and advantages that our discipline has to offer.

Lack of Knowledge of Work Environments

The role of student is not inherently good preparation for that of worker. Although some authority relationship does flow from teacher to student, that authority has become increasingly ambiguous and negotiable over time. Yes, faculty set the curriculum, decide what activities to feature, and evaluate students' performance. However, the past few decades have seen growing emphasis placed on students as consumers who expect to have a voice in the content and form of their education. Millennials and Generation Z also are fighting for greater and more meaningful voices in the workplace, but the power of workers is limited, particularly in aspiring for promotion within the organizational hierarchy. Students may also be more likely to accept at face value organizational claims to democratic and cooperative leadership, the truth of which may be disputable. My students with work experience often express surprise and frustration over how managers invite them to be critical and provide suggestions for work improvements, but become defensive when they offer their positive criticism. And of course, students may not know how to present that criticism to fit organizational norms. Academic criticism is more direct and heated than what is appropriate in other environments. Sociology curriculum can and should prepare students better to approach these differences in culture.

Employability and Sociology

This book uses the concept of employability as a basis for integrating the content, methods, and history of Sociology with the more mundane issues that you and your fellow students may need to prepare for the labor market. Universities and their critics tend to define employability very narrowly, often confusing imperfect measures with the concept itself. For example, universities sometimes define employability simply as graduation rates (Kirp, 2019). Other definitions emphasize social mobility and earning potential (Education, 2019) or straightforward return on investment (Mangan, 2019). Such outcomes-oriented definitions are atomistic and inaccurate. Universities cannot and should not be responsible for specific jobs or incomes; their responsibility is to impart the processes that facilitate them. Employability in this context is used broadly to encompass the capacity to start, develop, manage, and change careers that fit Sociology graduates' personal and professional goals. It focuses on three key dimensions: pre-professional identity, transferable skills, and career management (Harvey, 2001; Bridgstock, 2009; Jackson, 2016). Each demands a unique form of recontextualization. The formation of a pre-professional identity requires an exploration of the discipline's normative elements with an eye toward integrating them into the individual identity of students. Sociology is rich in transferable skills (Ciabattari et al., 2018), but those skills must be recontextualized so that you can express them in the content and format that employers use. The language of Sociology is not the language of employers, and you must calibrate your communications accordingly. Careful language is especially crucial during the job application process. Sociology also offers concrete knowledge related to career management, through its study of organizations, networks, entrepreneurship, and other areas of concentration. However, this knowledge is rarely discussed in terms of how it can be adapted to foster personal needs. A description of how these three dimensions will be covered in this book's 12 short chapters follows.

Part I. Pre-professional Identity

Persistent issues residing deep within sociological knowledge tend to interfere with recontextualizing Sociology in a way that addresses employers' needs. Sociology's obsession with defining itself as a science has kept us from explicitly exploring the subject of developing a sociological identity and has precluded us from considering the identity needs of undergraduate students and their future challenges. This section of the book attempts to remedy this oversight by offering a guide for how to create a professional, sociological identity. Chapter 2 explores the content and methods that Sociology offers as foundations for developing this professional identity as undergraduates and what elements must be nurtured individually. Sociology offers a clear point of view, but each individual must add their own action orientations in order to acquire a viable, sustainable identity. Chapter 3 uncovers the values and norms implicit in sociological content and provides some practical examples for how to transform them into a code of conduct. Chapters 4 and 5 concentrate on relationship building both as part of a professional identity and as sources of self-discovery and career opportunities. Chapter 4 explores finding and building supportive communities, and Chap. 5 focuses on networking as a tool for career advancement.

Part II. Transferable Skills

The Sociology major curriculum helps develop a wide variety of skills and expertise. As Sociology undergraduates, you need to recognize the additional skills you have developed either through your personal life or through your degree work in general classes and electives. This section of the book offers a guide for recontextualizing your skills using the conventions employers have created. The main tools of this recontextualization are the resume and the cover letter. Chapter 6 provides a general overview of the resume and its components, offering a sociological perspective on its structure and content. Chapter 7 concentrates on identifying the skills and expertise developed by the Sociology major and suggests how to communicate your sociological self in the resume to your best advantage. Chapter 8 deals with extracurricular activities and how to use the language of business to emphasize employability.

Part III. Career Management

Sociological knowledge can unquestionably contribute to career management. The literature on Work and Occupations, Economic Sociology, as well as Organizational Studies offers a variety of information about the challenges of work organizations and labor markets. I would recommend that all Sociology students take classes in these areas, but I know that not all programs offer them on a regular basis. Assuming a lack of this knowledge, this part of the book provides a basic overview of sociological knowledge that may be useful for making the transition from school to work. Chapter 9 recommends how to combine elements of your professional identity with the skills identified in the previous chapters to search and apply for jobs. This chapter includes how to write a cover letter. Chapter 10 uses the sociological imagination to explore the history and culture of managerial sciences to help prepare for workplace issues you may encounter. Chapter 11 concentrates on the first interaction you are likely to have with managerial culture: the job selection process. Finally, Chap. 12 describes some of the realities of organizational behavior that may clash with one's personal and sociological values and lays out strategies for resolving them.

Limitations and Cautionary Notes

I started thinking about career development curriculum for sociologists around 2017. Since then, I have seen many students successfully identify and "sell" Sociology as an asset. This book encapsulates my experiences trying to bridge the gap between traditional academic Sociology, students' interests and goals, and the demands of labor markets and work organizations. It is very much a work of applied Sociology. Within this practical, applied approach, I take liberties with the content that may not be suitable in more scientific or critical contexts. Some faculty and students may criticize me as contributing to capitalism and managerialism. They may feel that by teaching how to approach and navigate existing labor markets and organizations, I am perpetuating the imperfect systems that Sociology criticizes. I recognize this challenge, but I am writing this as a book of adaptation, not revolution. Working toward a better society will require you to learn how to consciously integrate yourself into and navigate systems that Sociology professors have spent their lives criticizing—all of which you will hopefully manage without losing sight of your original goals and dedication or your faith in the power of political participation, collective action, and public policies to create better systems. Understanding the systems provides a guide to effective action. By making the content uncompromisingly sociological and critical, I hope to gird you with the tools necessary to navigate the system while retaining your sociological self in the process. In other words, I want to help you choose your battles wisely. To coin a phrase, don the hat when you must, but avoid the Kool-Aid!

In defining the problem of career development as one of recontextualization, this work also follows the tradition of Public Sociology. It provides language tools to help bridge the cultural gaps with employers. This language provides you with the potential to become an effective ambassador for the discipline you have studied. With this goal in mind, I have tried to keep the technical language to a minimum while showing how sociological concepts apply. Concepts listed include where you can go to further explore topics if desired. Most importantly, I introduce what I call the "language of management." Language can be both limiting and empowering. While the language of business can and is used to manipulate workers, workers also can use it to achieve their goals. Finally, the parts of this book that fall into the more critical tradition are directed toward internal consumption by Sociology faculty and students, not employers or other audiences. All disciplines, practices, and technologies have advantages and disadvantages, meaningful purposes, and unintended consequences. Individuals attracted to those disciplines love them as much as we who teach it love Sociology. Criticism, even if it is scientifically and empirically supported, is not a useful tool for building bridges.

In addition to the public and applied paradigms, this book represents a personal endeavor. The content is based on my academic, advising, and individual experiences. You will no doubt notice certain biases. You will detect a sense of urgency and fatalism regarding existing opportunities; this sense of urgency may not apply to your personal circumstances. Ambition also permeates these pages. I want you and all Sociology students to "take over the world;" you deserve it. I also believe that sociologists in positions of power can be a transformational force for the betterment of society. Just as this book is a personal endeavor, each reader's career development journey is personal and unique. *My* ambition does not have to be *your* ambition. The book includes examples, content, and advice from other Sociology students representing a myriad of paths. Hopefully, you can find information in these pages that fits your interests and goals. If nothing else, you will find activities that lead you through a cycle of reflection and action for identifying and achieving your aims. Employability is not static; it must be constantly developed and affirmed in the face of changing circumstances. I hope this book provides you with a good start on a rich and satisfying lifelong journey.

Works Cited

Addo, F. R., Houle, J. N., & Sassler, S. (2019). The changing nature of the association between student loan debt and marital behavior in young adulthood. *Journal of Family and Economic Issues, 40*(1), 86–101.

Bridgstock, R. (2009). The graduate attributes we've overlooked: Enhancing graduate employability through career management skills. *Higher Education Research & Development, 28*(1), 31–44.

Ciabattari, T., Lowney, K. S., Monson, R. A., Senter, M. S., & Chin, J. (2018). Linking sociology majors to labor market success. *Teaching Sociology, 46*(3), 191–207.

Education, C. o. H. (2019). Special report: Six emerging trends you need to know about. Retrieved from https://www.chronicle.com/interactives/horizon on December 3, 2022.

Elliott, W., & Lewis, M. (2015). Student debt effects on financial well-being: Research and policy implications. *Journal of Economic Surveys, 29*(4), 614–636.

Friedman, Z. (2021, February 20). Student loan debt statistics in 2021: A record $1.7 trillion. *Forbes*. Retrieved from https://www.forbes.com/sites/zackfriedman/2021/02/20/student-loan-debt-statistics-in-2021-a-record-17-trillion/?sh=13fddd691431 on December 11, 2022.

Hanson, M. (2022). Average cost of college by year. Retrieved from https://educationdata.org/average-cost-of-college-by-year on December 6, 2022.

Harvey, L. (2001). Defining and measuring employability. *Quality in Higher Education, 7*(2), 97–109.

Houle, J. N., & Warner, C. (2017). Into the red and back to the nest? Student debt, college completion, and returning to the parental home among young adults. *Sociology of Education, 90*(1), 89–108.

Jackson, D. (2016). Re-conceptualising graduate employablity: The importance of pre-professional identity. *HIgher Education Research & Development, 35*(5), 925–939.

Kim, C., & Sakamoto, A. (2008). The rise of intra-occupational wage inequality in the United States, 1983 to 2002. *American Sociological Review, 73*(1), 129–157.

Kim, C., Tamborini, C. R., & Sakamoto, A. (2015). Field of study in college and lifetime earnings in the United States. *Sociology of Education, 88*(4), 320–339.

Kirp, D. (2019). *The college dropout scandal.* Oxford University Press.

Mangan, K. (2019). *Everyone wants to measure the value of college. Now the gates foundation wants a say.* Chronicle of Higher Education. Retrieved from https://www.chronicle.com/article/Everyone-Wants-to-Measure-the/246301/ on December 2, 2022.

Mezza, A., Ringo, D., Sherlund, S., & Sommer, K. (2020). Student loans and homeownership. *Journal of Labor Economics, 38*(1), 215–260.

NACE. (2022). *Salary survey: Starting salary projection for class of 2022 new college graduates.* National Association of Colleges and Employers.

NCES, N. C. f. E. S. (2016–2017). Digest of educational statistics. Tables on bachelor degrees (322.20, 322.30,322.40). Retrieved from https://nces.ed.gov/programs/digest/2018menu_tables.asp on December 3, 2022.

NCES, N. C. f. E. S. (2022). *Price for attending an undergraduate institution*. Condition of Education. Retrieved from https://nces.ed.gov/programs/coe/indicator/cua on December 11, 2022

Roberts, K. A., & Donahue, K. A. (2000). Professing professionalism: Bureaucratization and deprofessionalization in the academy. *Sociological Focus, 33*(4), 365–383.

RTI, I. (2019). First-generation college students: Demographic characteristics and postsecondary enrollment. Retrieved from https://firstgen.naspa.org/files/dmfile/FactSheet-01.pdf on November 29, 2022.

Stabile, D. (2007). *Economics, competition and academia: An intellectual history of sophism versus virtue*. Edward Elgar Publishing.

Tamborini, C. R., Kim, C., & Sakamoto, A. (2015). Education and lifetime earnings in the United States. *Demography, 52*(4), 1383–1407.

A Sociological Professional Identity

Sociologists have long been studying identity formation and its consequences. Identity is a form of internalization of cultural norms around specific groups, roles, and areas of social life. As members of complex societies, we have many overlapping identities. The sentence "I am an immigrant Latino mother" integrates and separates different identities that co-exist within one person. A professional identity is a particular type, defined as a work-related sense of self. While we tend to think about our work identities as separate from other parts of ourselves, in reality they are not. People decide to study particular majors and engage in certain occupations related to their personal characteristics, such as gender and ethnicity (Archer & Leathwood 2003; Moreau & Leathwood, 2006; Kirton, 2009). Sociology offers you opportunities to formally study your own identities and the systems that have affected your personal life.

Ideally, the process of forming a professional identity starts early in your college career. Done in tandem with your studies, it leads to the development of a pre-professional identity and a specialized work-related consciousness through self-reflection. This consciousness integrates the knowledge, skills, and values gained from studying Sociology with your personal disposition, interests, and goals. The addition of experiential learning helps you orient that consciousness toward problem solving. The process of identity formation, or reformation, continues through the transition from school to work and beyond; from their initial foundations, identities must adapt to changes in the work environment. Over time, this consciousness transforms itself into internalized structures that guide your evaluation of the world and your behavior, a concept that Bourdieu (2004) called "habitus." Through your classes, the sociological way of being is "deposited" or internalized. Professional identities and their corresponding habitus differ from other types of identity by their

© The Author(s), under exclusive license to Springer
Nature Switzerland AG 2023
M. A. Martinez, *The Employable Sociologist*,
https://doi.org/10.1007/978-3-031-41323-0_2

intentionality; they require explicit efforts of reflection, integration with your other existing identities, and recontextualization to accommodate the labor market and work organizations. Professional identities also enable you to visualize yourself as a future professional. A solid professional identity will help you develop the attitude toward your work that is appropriate to your goals; provide you with tools to weather the volatility of labor markets and organizations; cultivate a global-minded approach; and prepare you to operate in diverse workplaces under various contractual arrangements. It also provides the foundation for a career based on passion and lifelong learning. Much has been written about what constitutes an ideal professional identity, including some of these chief components:

1. Public and personal recognition of a legitimate professional identity (Holden & Hamblett, 2007);
2. Mastery of the knowledge, skills, values, and ideologies associated with the discipline and their application (Reid et al., 2008);
3. Reconciliation of personal values with those of the discipline and of future work organizations and jobs (Trede et al., 2012);
4. Sense of responsibility and purpose (Henkel, 2005);
5. Sense of membership and understanding of relationships and community (Hunter et al., 2007);
6. Knowledge of jobs, careers, organizations, and industries for potential employment as well as their culture (Trede et al., 2012).

Part I of the book illustrates the reflection/action process for integrating Sociology with your interests. This chapter will explore how the theory and methods of Sociology can provide a partial foundation for developing the content of your professional identity. The next chapter will examine the norms and values implicit within the practice of Sociology, followed by an investigation of what Sociology can tell us about relationship building in Chaps. 4 and 5. Identity formation will be addressed throughout the book, including the discussion of Transferable Skills in Part II and Career Management in Part III. Part II will offer help in recontextualizing your skills to fit the labor market, gaining greater awareness of their value and your own confidence in the process. Part III presents an overview of what Sociology knows about industries and workplaces and relates it to the goal of individual application.

The Professional Status of Sociology

Sociological theories, methods, and practice provide fertile ground for the creation of an undergraduate professional identity. However, Sociology also has clear disadvantages vis-à-vis other disciplines that should not be ignored. These disadvantages revolve around a lack of obvious public professional standing and the internalization of this lack—issues or perceptions of central import in managing the transition from school to work. Put frankly, people may not immediately recognize sociologists as professionals, leaving you to do the same. One of the realities facing a Sociology student is the lack of general acknowledgment of our status as a profession by many employers, parents, and other figures of authority. Fortunately, Sociology itself provides us with answers to the question of whether we can confidently claim our discipline as a profession. Sociology has a robust history in the study of professions as a socially constructed occupational category. Professions publicly claim that their work is different from that performed by other occupations—different meaning "superior." They base their superiority on three principles: rationality, merit, and public service (Hughes, 1958; Daniels, 1971). Professionals claim to have specialized knowledge and expertise not found generally in workers and managers. They contend that they develop and acquire those skills through a rigorous and rational process where only the most capable survive. Finally, they declare their intent to defend and promote the benefit of society even at the cost of personal self-interest. These principles of rationality, merit, and public service are supposed to transcend economic relationships. Under this logic, the professional role is so important that its functioning cannot be entrusted to market forces or individual organizational hierarchies. This book will make clear that Sociology, beginning at the undergraduate level, also fulfills these three requirements. Students of Sociology undergo training in a discipline based on scientific principles; we use these principles in identifying remedies for improving both societies and individuals.

Notwithstanding our having these constitutive earmarks of a profession, we sociologists lack some of the institutional and organizational mechanisms that other professionals such as doctors, lawyers, and accountants have formed to support their status. These mechanisms are not part of the essential nature of professions, but have produced coherent identities, evolved boundaries, and produced advantages in the market for their members. They are instrumental in projecting a professional identity to the public—one that commands high degrees of autonomy and remuneration. Some of these typical mechanisms are briefly described below.

Professional Associations Many professions form associations that establish educational and other standards as requisites for jobs. Sociology has a professional association, the American Sociological Association (ASA), but it is predominantly dedicated to the advancement of research and teaching. While this work benefits both students and faculty by improving the quality of our content and our pedagogies, it does little to promote Sociology students' contributions to the world. Occasionally, ASA crafts and publishes opinions on political and policy issues, but its influence and visibility are limited compared to other institutions like the American Medical Association, the American Bar Association, or the American Association of Finance and Accounting.

Consecration Mechanisms and Rituals Not long ago when only elites attended higher education institutions, the four years of study needed to get a bachelor's degree were considered enough to lay claim to certain levels of expertise and professional status. Rather than attending structured master's or PhD programs, graduates just continued studying while teaching. As higher education became more popular, new standards and degrees were created to "distinguish" those with superior knowledge. For sociologists, the big distinction is between those with or without a PhD, with only the latter having the generally acknowledged right to call themselves professionals. Some disciplines like Psychology insist on the need for a PhD to carry the title of "professional"; others do not have such a lofty requirement.

Enforced Licensing Some professional associations set standards delimiting participation in their fields and partner with the government to assure their enforcement. Federal and state governments develop and enforce licensing mechanisms that are dependent on ambiguous consecration mechanisms. Through this process, the associations control both the demand and supply for their services (Brockman, 1962; Hamowy, 1979; P. A. Mills & Young, 1999). Sociology, of course, lacks this arrangement.

Symbols of Membership Because Sociology professionals define ourselves by our way of thinking, we have not developed physical manifestations of our identities. Doctors have lab coats and lawyers have expensive suits to help identify them. Accountants can usually be identified by the instruments of their profession: once calculators and pencils, now computer software. Individuals trained in Sociology have limited opportunities to interact with others besides academic conferences.

We need the t-shirt to help us define our professional identity both figuratively and physically.

Specialized Career Track Good luck finding a job posting that includes the word Sociology. The undergraduate Sociology curriculum is not designed to place majors in specific applied careers or to engage in specific types of social action (Spalter-Roth et al., 2010). That means that neither society nor professors will provide you with a clear path. As a professional, that task falls on each individual to decide what kind of actions and careers are best suited to their knowledge and potential and what means will best advance their goals and improve society. The lack of exclusive career paths for sociologists does not diminish the rationality of those actions or the importance of that knowledge. Sociology just happens to be useful in broader environments than other professions.

Market Rewards Sociological literature on professions observes that licensing and consecration requirements translate into market benefits like higher salaries and exclusive access to positions for those who make it. As mentioned in the Introduction, sociologists do not have such market advantages. In fact, we are in direct competition with other majors that have a more recognized professional identity.

Public Prestige One criterion for determining whether an area of inquiry or study is a profession is public recognition. The general media, in particular television, have created a mystique around certain professions, like medicine and law. Accountants have less visibility, but they benefit from the conventional understanding that their quantitative work denotes a higher intelligence deserving of higher status.

If listing these mechanisms utilized by certain professions prompts any conclusion, it is that Sociology students have all the responsibilities of a professional without any of the social advantages. Our identity is based on rationality and centered on caring for others (Clouder, 2005). Not surprisingly, many Sociology students have problems defining themselves as professionals. Yet, social recognition is a welcome but not necessary condition for the creation of a professional identity. Being a professional is a matter of habitus, which entails developing behaviors and dispositions. You *are* a professional if you *believe* you are and behave accordingly. That behavior carries real consequences, including a boost in your confidence if nothing else. This positive effect is independent of whatever advantages external processes produce.

The Undergraduate Sociological Identity

My first step in preparing to write this book was to conduct a bibliographic search for any mentions of the sociological identity in scholarly journals. I found a fair amount of literature on that topic, but no articles about a sociological identity for undergraduates. They all centered on academic research and teaching, and mostly provided guidance on how to construct a career in academia for those with a PhD. A couple pieces dealt with using the concept to integrate part-time adjunct faculty into the profession. Even texts related to career development for undergraduate sociologists did not explore or mention the concept.

Given the centrality of a professional identity for employability, this lack of discussion is worrisome but by no means accidental. Many Sociology faculty define the discipline as an exclusively scientific research endeavor that sometimes includes teaching. In this view, the only professional sociologists are those employed by universities. This is the position of C. Wright Mills (1959), author of one of the most influential works on the practice of Sociology. He defined the boundaries of Sociology and its most accepted definition in terms of a concept he called the sociological imagination whereby individual problems can be explained by societal troubles. This theory strongly emphasizes the role of historical processes in explaining current social contexts. While it has provided a clear path for the continuing development of the discipline, emphasis on the sociological imagination has resulted in narrowing the profession to exclude all but research and teaching. Sociology is something that happens in universities, done by individuals with the advantage of tenure able to offer up critical analysis shielded from the general forces of societal domination and exploitation. C. Wright Mills had extraordinarily little to say about the undergraduate students that he sent into the world. In his view, his obligation was solely to show them how to think. That renders Sociology undergraduates neither professionals nor sociologists in training. His position, of course, is a product of his era. He was writing during a time of high government redistribution, much of it directed toward expanding higher education as a source of social mobility. Jobs were plentiful and paid well. His attitude becomes untenable in "pay-your-own-way" twenty-first century America where job quality varies greatly.

Since Mills excluded undergraduates and other non-academics from the "work of Sociology," there have been attempts to broaden the definition of the discipline. The most influential, spearheaded by Michael Burawoy (2005), identifies four categories of Sociology

The Undergraduate Sociological Identity

1. Professional Sociology: theoretically organized empirical research conducted within research programs or non-academic departments;
2. Public Sociology: interaction with the extra-academic world, including efforts to improve the public image of Sociology, teaching, and textbook writing;
3. Critical Sociology: reflective self-examination of the discipline; a critique of theories, methods, and conclusions;
4. Policy Sociology: a defense of sociological research, funding, and human subjects in which sociologists are usually hired as contractors and advisors on a temporary basis.

Burawoy's main concern lies with Public Sociology. He views the relative lack of public recognition and influence as an existential problem facing the discipline. He worries that other fields with less rich and rigorous methods and content have more influence in public life. Still, his recommendations are directed toward traditional academic Sociology Departments by encouraging them to reward scholarly work aimed at general audiences. Burawoy explicitly mentions undergraduate students only within the Public Sociology role, and even then only as ambassadors of the discipline to the outside world. While being an ambassador is some improvement over not even being mentioned, the role is still incidental. Ambassadors are outside the social group they represent. Furthermore, if undergraduates are our ambassadors, we are sending them out to represent us without the tools needed for the job. We do not train them in how to recontextualize knowledge for general audiences.

Sociology curriculums and faculty attitudes must change to develop and strengthen students' professional identity and thus employability. Faculty need to treat students as professionals-in-training, and students need to see their behavior inside and outside the classroom as a reflection of the discipline they are studying. This novel approach can and should be based on the principles of sociological thinking, with the sociological imagination at its core. Students can use the sociological imagination in their career development efforts by inverting its logic. If individual problems can be explained by way of social troubles, social problems provide a foundation to explain the career development issues of Sociology undergraduates. This inversion makes the sociological point of view the foundational content of a professional identity and provides a guiding principle for curriculum development. As a starting point for the reflection process, I explore three elements: the sociological point of view as the strongest component of undergraduate professional identity, action orientations for undergraduate students to define for themselves outside their sociological training, and the impediments that our way of thinking may present in work environments.

The Sociological Point of View for Undergraduates

Besides believing and behaving as professionals, Sociology undergraduates need to identify and recontextualize the content of the curriculum and the actual meanings concerning that identity. What distinguishes sociologists from others is how we think. This method of thinking is conveyed and absorbed through Sociology classes and related academic work. At the conclusion of this training, Sociology becomes not only a point of view but a *personal* point of view; it becomes a personal epistemology, a set of assumptions about the nature, limits, and certainty of knowledge (Baxter Magolda, 2004). Those who have it become part of an epistemological community, people who see the world in the same terms. If you continue in academia as a professor, the application of this epistemology will extend into your research and teaching and will similarly mark your colleagues. In that situation, the content of your identity does not need recontextualizing.

If as an undergraduate you opt for a job in any of the many organizations and industries available outside academia, you will have to adapt your point of view to fit the unfamiliar environment. The biggest adaptation will be the need to replace empirical reasoning with heuristics. Reason requires extensive time and resources: time to think, resources to collect data, and time to engage in dialog between the two and produce conclusions. Outside academia, there is no time or resources for that sort of endeavor. You can still apply sociological thinking: it just needs to be simplified. Heuristics are practical methods of decision-making based on assumptions, in this case extracted from the theory and methods of Sociology. Heuristics are less normative and more instrumental; we use heuristics because they work, not because they are absolute truth (although most of us hope they are) or because they are morally right.

One aspect of Sociology is uncovering the assumptions regarding theories and methods, therefore making the work of identifying them familiar to all who study it. However, expressing such assumptions, consciously and without negative connotations, is another matter. Good practice of the scientific method makes you feel like you are always failing. That is not an attitude to bring to the outside world. Sociology is a complex body of knowledge that can inspire different and contradictory heuristics. When we use sociological assumptions as heuristics, we accept their truth and utilize them to make decisions. Sociology allows each person to tailor their own heuristics according to your needs. As a point of departure for this work, I've listed my own favorite sociological "heuristics," divided into three categories: the Nature of the World, the Nature of Knowledge, and the Nature of People, which I outline below.

Nature of the World

1. All social systems are human creations, and therefore can be improved.
2. Problems have multiple, complex causes.
3. Personal problems tend to reflect social troubles and failures.
4. Society has forces both of cooperation and competition.
5. What people perceive as truth has real consequences.

Nature of Knowledge

1. Knowledge is always incomplete and evolving.
2. Causes and contributing conditions differ.
3. Facts are value-neutral; otherwise, they are not facts.
4. The evaluation of facts is not value-neutral.
5. Correlation is not causation.
6. Representation and generalization are a necessary part of any truth.

Nature of People

1. Points of view and opinions are connected to social positions and group memberships.
2. Facts are never enough to explain values, beliefs, and opinions of people.
3. The behaviors of individuals can be partially explained by the external forces they face.
4. Behaviors are probabilistic in nature, and therefore can never be explained completely by science.
5. Individuals are both constrained and empowered by social relations.
6. People like order but feel oppressed by it.

You may recognize some of these elements and share them as part of your identity. Others you may find controversial or irrelevant. You may want to add your own sociological wisdom about the world. Don't expect fellow faculty and students to share all the ideas within your heuristics. For example, my own central heuristic is that people can only become rich by taking from those who produce wealth (or who produced it in the past). All wealth is based on exploitation. I apply this very Marxist heuristic in my dealings with managers. This position may be too radical for some, too materialistic for others. Regardless, it is the basis of my sociological identity and is a tool I use to guide my behaviors in the workplace.

For you, this list can be used as a resource for articulating your own epistemology. Decide which assumptions you agree with and which ones you want to employ in any decision-making situation. You may want to add other items to the sociological point of view that describes "you" as a sociologist. There are no right or wrong answers, only choices.

Action Orientations Comprising Your Identity

In another seminal development in the history of exploring the sociological identity, the German sociologist Max Weber articulated the main disconnect between teachers and students of Sociology. He held that teachers are focused on training students how to think, but students are looking for action, to make the world better. His original lecture on the topic took place in the early twentieth century, but the point still applies today. You will still hear Sociology faculty say that what students do with sociological knowledge is not their concern. In reality, although Sociology has expended considerable effort in explaining actions (Parsons & van Ham, 1937), the discipline provides no blueprint for what to do with such knowledge; it lacks a theory of Sociology in action. Completing your professional identity as a Sociology major requires you to bring, explore, and define your own action orientation. This exercise in self-authoring (Baxter Magolda, 2004) is something that nobody can tell you how to define. But once defined, this action orientation can help you narrow your job options.

In my position advising undergraduate Sociology majors, I try to help students define their "action selves." These "roles" provide a shorthand for categorizing action types. As with the sociological point of view, my list is neither exhaustive nor universally accepted. It offers titles and descriptions that may be useful in constructing and expressing the action component of your identity. You may be inclined to mix different action types or create a new type. That is expected. My suggested action types and what motivates them include:

Scientists The main motivation of a scientist is to find truth through reason and empiricism. The scientist in its purest form is only vaguely interested in improving the world. In his/her view, truth is a precursor to social change, but the work of implementing it is left to others.

Educators Their passion is to share information with and develop the skills of others. They feel committed to create capable and knowledgeable workers and citizens for society. They also see their job as a tool to empower individuals to achieve their own personal goals.

Mentors More individually oriented than the teacher, they tend to enjoy and seek one-on-one social interactions. They want to understand the needs of individuals and provide specific guidance for achieving goals. They deal with the more personal consequences of an environment or experience and uncover hidden elements and assumptions.

Artists This type of person uses their skills and imagination to express or communicate ideas through different forms of visual or other media. Combined with sociological knowledge, this expression of Sociology projects a mirror of social issues and problems. My favorite sociologist/artist is Oscar-winning director Bong Joon-ho. He was a Sociology major in his native Korea and I often use his movies as illustrations of sociological theories. His movies *Parasite* (2019) and *Snowpiercer* (2013) are both impressive pieces of art using the sociological imagination to denounce inequality and its consequences.

Activists This personality type wants to force institutions to radically transform themselves. They usually identify discrimination, domination, and exploitation as the root causes of all social evils and problems. Activists wish to create bottom-up transformations and to promote community participation and democratic values.

Advocates Focused on social change as much as the activist, the advocate is more aware of complexities in social problems and the need to intervene at various levels of social organization: individual, family, community, and government. Sociologists with this orientation connect people with resources by becoming social workers and social service providers in governments and nonprofits. Many of this type work for schools and universities in roles that improve educational opportunities.

Organizers Students with this profile are usually geared toward understanding and creating systems to achieve social goals. They tend to be attracted to order and reason. A sociological education balances the abstract thinking of the organizer with a preoccupation with understanding how systems affect individuals and communities beyond their narrow goal.

Reformers/Improvers This action orientation is similar to the organizer's profile but has a more conservative bent. The reformer considers the needs of systems and tries to improve them without disrupting their functions. As with the organizer, having a sociological orientation makes the reformer more aware, able, and willing to modify systems in a way that minimizes negative consequences.

Community Builders This problem-solving type wants people to enjoy the emotional, physical, and material benefits of social interaction. Activities appealing to those with this orientation may include event planning, management of community spaces (such as a store or a coffee shop), socially conscious publicity efforts, and engagement positions in cultural institutions.

Mediators This role specializes in the building and maintenance of relationships that have both common and adversarial goals. For example, many for-profit organizations have complicated relationships with the communities they inhabit; they bring them both advantages and negative consequences. The mediator attempts to balance the needs of the organization with those of the community to achieve mutually beneficial goals.

Communicators This role is focused on the creation and distribution of informational content adapted for targeted audiences and media platforms. It includes writing and editing in different formats, social media postings, and presentation design. Their products can have informational or motivational purposes. Graphic designers and video and podcast producers straddle the line between artist and communicator.

Strategists/Thought Leaders Individuals with this bent are always looking for new and interesting ideas in diverse areas of knowledge. They push themselves and others to apply those ideas to improve social systems and communities. This action type can be combined with others and practiced in any role or job. These are clear innovators who promote alternative ways of action and find jobs in diverse areas such as journalism, teaching, and management.

Vulnerabilities of Sociologists

A vital component of any professional identity is self-criticism. Who we choose to be has advantages and disadvantages. Being aware of the vulnerabilities, limits, and disadvantages within our thinking helps protect us from manipulation and exploitation. While sociological theories and methods provide problem-solving tools either in the form of science or heuristics, the discipline also provides identity elements that may put us at a disadvantage compared to other professionals. Many of these elements stem from the fact that we see Sociology as a science rather than a practice. Others are related to Sociology's anti-capitalist and critical bent, which may not be appropriate within a work organization. Some of the disadvantages of a sociologist are described next.

A Tendency to Be Overly Idealistic

In my experience, students attracted to Sociology are highly moral and ethical people. They want to do the right thing, and they want to know what the right thing is. Our inability to "perfectly" follow our ideals in the face of systems outside our control may lead to disillusionment and cynicism. In the end, no individual or society perfectly fulfills the full promise of its values. We are human, we fail. We owe ourselves the same empathy and care that we want to show others. While our instincts may orient us toward helping other people, we must not become martyrs in the process. Although we do not study self-interest, we need to make sure that we also consider ourselves in making our plans and decisions.

Oversocialized World View

There are two potential mistakes in taking the oversocialized approach, particularly when applied to a personal and professional life. First, it may lead us to believe that since there is little we can do about the general health of society, nothing matters and that nihilism absolves us from responsibilities toward others. Nihilism is incompatible with the sociological approach. The second mistake is to have such strict standards of behavior for ourselves and others that we isolate ourselves from the benefits of social interaction. For a personal sociological identity, Granovetter's (1985) approach to society as a source of both constraints and opportunities is more conducive to effective action. It is true that culture and structure constrain us, but they also give us opportunities to act. We should be able and willing to decide what actions are best for ourselves and others within the limits of ethics. It is important to remember that you have options and can make new options for yourself and others.

Guilt over Privilege and Power

Inequality is an undeniable fact of modern and neoliberal societies. A few individuals have obscenely great amounts of power and privilege in all dimensions (think Bill Gates or Donald Trump); many more have little to none (undocumented laborers, for example). Outside these extremes, however, we all are exploited and exploit each other. As the heuristics lists showed, modern societies are extraordinarily complex. Such complexity leads to a distribution of privilege and power based on a variety of dimensions, some ascriptive (such as gender, race, age, and parental and maternal education) and some developed (education or income). Privilege is a relative term. Take my case. I am a woman, Latina, an immigrant, a first-generation college graduate, but I have a PhD, I have tenure in a major American university, and my income is slightly above the median for my community. While you may think that my privileges come from merit, the reality is that I also have a skin color pale enough that people on the street consider me white. "Colorism" has eased my way compared to colleagues with darker skin. Chances are you have privileges, or at the very least will develop some by finishing a college degree. As you continue on your chosen career and personal paths, you will develop some privileges and will also have to exercise some form of power over others. While privilege and power should be acknowledged, you should not feel guilty about them or let guilt interfere with your goals. Remember that systemic changes are the only way to abolish privilege. We individuals can use that privilege and power to help those around us.

A Tendency to Analyze Instead of Act

When I was growing up, I heard a Mexican comedian do a stand-up routine about the differences in behavior between Americans and Mexicans. One joke focused on their different approaches to problem solving: while Americans hurried to implement solutions—any solution regardless of effectiveness—Mexicans spent all their time analyzing the problem and never actually "doing" anything about it. Sociologists fall firmly into the longtime analyzers camp. One of the most difficult lessons to learn in the process of transitioning from school to work is that employees are paid to *do*, not think. Taking time to think about the correct action may be preferable, but eventually you must do something. Ideally, you will finish your work within the timeframe your boss requires. Similarly, expect to find that at work people spend less time discussing issues than students do in the classroom. As your career progresses, you will be more likely to accept systems without questioning them, just because you are familiar with them. Beware of this tendency so that you can avoid it. Maintaining an identity as a sociologist includes managing expectations regarding reflection and action.

Conclusion

Having a strong and stable professional identity is a key component of employability. You form a professional identity by integrating common elements based on the discipline you studied, your personal interests, values, and orientations, and the demands of work environments. This process starts in the classroom and continues throughout your career. As Sociology majors you enter the work arena knowing you will face a number of specific obstacles, including a lack of public recognition of Sociology as a profession, a lack of mechanisms to create market advantages, and our discipline's own narrow definition limiting a professional sociologist to that of an academic. Recognizing the obstacles that come with sociological thinking is part of the process involved in shaping a professional identity of your own. Sociological theory and methods provide the foundation to create personal heuristics to help guide your decision-making in the context of work organizations. Developing your own "action" profile is an important part of forming your identity as a professional.

Discussion Questions

1. Think of your favorite sociology class(es). What assumptions about the nature of the world, the nature of knowledge, or the nature of people were established in the class?
2. Do you feel like a professional?

3. Mention action orientations not included in this chapter.
4. Think of two sociology professors. What action orientations do they have?
5. Think of two professors outside Sociology. What action orientations do they have?

Action/Reflection Activity

1. Determine three elements of your sociological identity using the following:
   (a) Heuristics that guide how you see the world
   (b) Your action orientation
   (c) What transformation or outcome you want to bring to society
   (d) Your vulnerabilities
2. Integrate those elements into an "elevator pitch" or brand statement of one or two short paragraphs.
3. Share your statement with other Sociology students to get their feedback. Write a second draft of your brand statement based on their observations.
4. Share your brand statement with somebody you trust who is not a sociologist (a family member, advisor, mentor) and ask for feedback. What do they understand by the statement? How could you make it better or clearer? Revise your brand statement a third time.

Works Cited

Archer, L., & Leathwood, C. (2003). Identities, inequalities and higher education. *Higher Education and Social Class: Issues of Exclusion and Inclusion*, 171–191.

Baxter Magolda, M. B. (2004). Evolution of a constructivist conceptualization of epistemological reflection. *Educational Psychologist, 39*(1), 31–42.

Bourdieu, P. (2004). Outline of the theory of practice: Structures and the habitus. In *Practicing history* (pp. 193–212). Routledge.

Brockman, N. C. (1962). The history of the American Bar association: A bibliographic essay. *The American Journal of Legal History, 6*(3), 269–285. https://doi.org/10.2307/844073

Burawoy, M. (2005). For public sociology. *American Sociological Review, 70*(1), 4–28.

Clouder, L. (2005). Caring as a 'threshold concept': Transforming students in higher education into health (care) professionals. *Teaching in Higher Education, 10*(4), 505–517.

Daniels, A. K. (1971). How free should professionals be? In E. Friedson (Ed.), *The professions and their prospects* (pp. 39-57). Sage Publications.

Granovetter, M. (1985). Economic action and social structure: The problem of embeddedness. *American Journal of Sociology, 91*(3), 481–510.

Works Cited

Hamowy, R. (1979). The early development of medical licensing laws in the United States. *The Journal of Libertarian Studies, 3*, 73.

Henkel, M. (2005). Academic identity and autonomy in a changing policy environment. *Higher Education, 49*(1–2), 155–176.

Higgs, J. (1993). Physiotherapy, professionalism and self-directed learning. *Journal of the Singapore Physiotherapy Association, 14*(1), 8–11.

Holden, R., & Hamblett, J. (2007). The transition from higher education into work: Tales of cohesion and fragmentation. *Education+Training, 49*(7), 516–585.

Hughes, E. C. (1958). *Men and their work*. Free Press.

Hunter, A. B., Laursen, S. L., & Seymour, E. (2007). Becoming a scientist: The role of undergraduate research in students' cognitive, personal, and professional development. *Science Education, 91*(1), 36–74.

Kirton, G. (2009). Career plans and aspirations of recent black and minority ethnic business graduates. *Work, Employment and Society, 23*(1), 12–29.

Mills, P. A., & Young, J. J. (1999). From contract to speech: The courts and CPA licensing laws 1921–1996. *Accounting, Organizations and Society, 24*(3), 243–262. https://doi.org/10.1016/S0361-3682(98)00042-7

Moreau, M. P., & Leathwood, C. (2006). Graduates' employment and the discourse of employability: A critical analysis. *Journal of Education and Work, 19*(4), 305–324.

Parsons, T., & van Ham, D. J. (1937). *The structure of social action*. McGraw Hill.

Pong, Masterson, K., Jeong, T., Nam, S., Pak, C., Lee, T. H., Evans, C., Song, K., Swinton, T., Bell, J., Spencer, O., Bremner, E., Ko, A., Hurt, J., Harris, E., Beltrami, M., & Lob, J. (2013). *Snowpiercer*. Anchor Bay Entertainment.

Pong, Kwak, S., Moon, Y., Han, C., Song, K., Yi, S., Cho, Y., Ch'oe, U., & Pak, S. (2019). *Parasite*. Kanopy.

Reid, A., Dahlgren, L. O., Petocz, P., & Dahlgren, M. A. (2008). Identity and engagement for professional formation. *Studies in Higher Education, 33*(6), 729–742.

Spalter-Roth, R., Senter, M. S., Stone, P., & Wood, M. (2010). ASA's bachelor's and beyond survey: Findings and their implications for students and departments. *Teaching Sociology, 38*(4), 314–329.

Trede, F., Macklin, R., & Bridges, D. (2012). Professional identity development: A review of the higher education literature. *Studies in Higher Education, 37*(3), 365–384.

Wright Mills, C. (1959). *The sociological imagination*. Oxford University Press.

The Values of Sociology

3

Norms and values to guide behaviors and decisions inside and outside the workplace form an indispensable part of any professional identity. To be considered a professional community, we sociologists need to emphasize what makes us different from those who study other topics. Norms and values can be expressed with different levels of abstraction and applicability. What we normally call values are concepts like liberty, solidarity (in its non-sociological meaning), fairness, equality, altruism, generosity, and sustainability. These concepts are so general that people can reach opposite definitions of what they mean in practice. At the other end of the spectrum are statements of specific application that grow into guidelines or rules to follow. For traditional professional occupations, the more specific norms and values are formalized into Codes of Conduct. Doctors have their own ethical conduct code based on the Hippocratic Oath. Accountants and lawyers have specific Codes of Conduct too. Just as the professions themselves, these guidelines are a product of modernity and an attempt to formalize "rational" norms and values. They are inclined toward the legalistic and a concern for punitive actions and criminal repercussions.

For sociologists, the American Sociological Association has a Code of Ethics and a committee in charge of hearing complaints about violations, which can be read here: https://www.asanet.org/sites/default/files/asa_code_of_ethics-june2018a.pdf. This code is very much oriented toward academics and their specific roles in teaching, research, and consulting. Its main concerns are fraud and misrepresentation of expertise. Provisions regarding diversity and anti-discrimination efforts tend to be overly specific; they center on the hiring of professors and the ethics of research. Beyond these topics, the content does not provide any guidance about how to behave in society as a sociologist.

© The Author(s), under exclusive license to Springer
Nature Switzerland AG 2023
M. A. Martinez, *The Employable Sociologist*,
https://doi.org/10.1007/978-3-031-41323-0_3

A single Code of Conduct is of little help to Sociology majors. The variety of potential jobs, occupations, organizations, and industries in which you will work encompasses multiple and complex ethical concerns. A single code inevitably ignores the richness, diversity, usefulness, and inspirational qualities of Sociology. Instead of a Code of Conduct, we should reflect on the deep history and intellectual tradition of Sociology and create a Statement of Values and Goals, an operating guide not directed toward specific and legalistic behavior, but to serve as a source of inspiration and intent for conduct in our professional and personal lives. This chapter attempts to tease out the often-hidden elements of Sociology that provide ethical guidance that might inform such a Statement of Values and Goals. The suggestions focus on practical goals and language easily understandable to those without sociological knowledge. They will be useful both in guiding your personal actions throughout your career and in explaining to general audiences what makes sociologists unique: our knowledge-based ethics.

Uncovering the Ethics of Sociology

By nature, Sociology students tend to be profoundly ethical and well-intentioned; they care about the world. They want to use the knowledge and skills they have gained through their studies to improve society. Occasionally, this sense of responsibility crosses into guilt. Talking to students about their career options, I've been struck with how many worry about disappointing faculty with their career choices. Recently, a student who wanted to become a franchisee of a local coffee chain apologized for his choice. Another, who was interested in becoming an academic, thought that she could not study Latinos because she was white. A student interested in Public Relations worried that joining a for-profit company represented failure, and an alumna working in a social service organization did not want to accept a promotion because it would mean becoming an "evil" manager.

Sometimes their sense of guilt comes from their admiration for faculty and their work. It is normal for students to regard faculty as examples of ethical sociologists. But what do Sociology faculty want from students? We want you to think sociologically is often the answer. But is that all? Although we may not say it explicitly, most faculty recognize that you must live and find happiness (if not success) in a world filled with constraints and obstacles. Some faculty place a high premium on research-related careers in academic settings. For them, anything else represents failure. Such attitudes ignore the facts that academia is being downsized and offers fewer opportunities; getting the chance to pursue a traditional research-oriented academic career is becoming akin to winning the lottery. As much as we emphasize critical thinking, we do not expect you to become a true revolutionary, Che Guevara style. We know that you will likely have to join organizations and participate in systems embedded in a capitalistic, postmodern, postindustrial society.

Can Sociology give you practical advice about how to act in the world if you don't end up doing research? In the classroom, we discuss Sociology as a science. We see sociological knowledge and theories as ways to describe and study reality. Sociology tells you what is (positive knowledge) instead of what should be (normative knowledge). If there is a normative component studied in the classroom, it is probably related to how our science should be practiced and how we should treat people while doing research. One benefit of studying Sociology is knowing that implicit culture is as real as explicit culture. Sociology is not exempted from norms and values that go beyond the scientific method, even if we fail to formally state them. In fact, our science offers clear ideas of how societies should be and how individuals should behave in them. These guidelines are already part of your identity as a sociologist but may assume the form of assumptions you take for granted rather than specific rules of behavior. In the classroom you may also have heard them framed more in the context of what governments or collectivities can and should do and less in terms of your own individual decisions.

Value neutrality and its less virtuous cousin, bias recognition, are the main values of any science, Sociology included. True value neutrality has been found to be impossible in all scientific endeavors. Sociology can aspire to objectivity, but can never achieve it. Our conclusions about the nature of social dynamics become theory, and those theories become the foundation of political ideology. Those of us who practice Sociology in the twenty-first century tend to gravitate toward certain theories out of our pre-existing political leanings. Theory and ideology are therefore intimately connected. For those interested in the connection between ideology and sociological theory, I recommend the book *Ideology and the Development of Social Theory* by Irving M. Zeitlin (2001) which covers the role of ideology in Sociology from early social thinkers like Montesquieu and Rousseau through the mid-twentieth century work of Herbert Mead. Using Zeitlin's account, I find the following three main values of Sociology most pertinent to the concerns of undergraduates:

Truth Most of your professors will tell you that our theories and methods are what make Sociology unique. This implies that they lead us to "true" knowledge of the social world. We define truth as the outcome of reason (theory) and empiricism (methods). While the way in which truth is achieved has remained constant, we have expanded our definition of the *nature* of truth. For example, American pragmatism introduced the idea of the truth of perception, the notion that what people believe has "real" consequences and is therefore a type of truth. We have also accepted the truth of experience, whereby only those who have experienced a phenomenon can possess a certain type of knowledge about it.

Cooperative Order The fundamental assumption of Sociology is that society and social organization are essential elements of human experience. We need each other; we need to find ways to organize ourselves to reach agreements on how to live together and divide the labor of production and reproduction. The ideas of mechanic and organic solidarity developed by Durkheim (1893) in his work, *The Social Division of Labor,* have become so universally accepted that we no longer even question them.

Emancipation The study of social systems includes their negative consequences. Cooperative orders vary in the degree to which they constrain both communities and individuals. Some social orders are repressive. Definitions of emancipation usually emphasize freedom from restrictions. Sociology's view of emancipation is more complex, evaluating systems that help groups and individuals achieve their potential and goals as positive. Emancipation is more than just not getting in the way; it is a system that actively makes it easier to achieve goals.

These fundamental values of Sociology provide you with means for developing more practical, personal behavioral goals. Truth is a concept both strong and flexible. It tells you clearly what is "not truth" and is able to accommodate multiple types of knowledge. Cooperative order and emancipation balance each other. While cooperation and emancipation are not opposed theoretically, in practice social systems tend to exchange one for the other. The right balance of cooperative order to emancipation is the content of political ideologies. However, your quest is not about politics, but about personal values and goals. The Statement of Values and Goals I envision provides the specific application of values. It should be a guide for individual behavior and a way to explain to the rest of the world how sociologists can contribute to their organizations and communities. An appropriate Statement of Values and Goals for sociologists, regardless of their jobs, comprises four main components: (1) behaviors to promote, (2) behaviors to avoid, (3) sociopolitical responsibilities, and (4) economic responsibilities. Using these dimensions, I came up with my own Statement of Goals and Values comprised of 14 elements. I hope that my own attempt at articulating ethical behaviors in my context will help you create your own. Each section of this chapter will explore how, given the history of the discipline and my own interpretation of that history, Sociology provides a basis for constructing concrete normative statements to guide ethical behavior. When pertinent, commentary about the conditions and obstacles alumni may face in applying those goals to the world outside academia will also be included.

Behaviors to Promote

Sociology is a social science born of the Enlightenment, modernity, and Western thinking. One can write and find umpteen volumes on the history and definition of modernity (Giddens, 1990), but for our purposes we will define it as a way of thinking, organizing, and living that emphasizes rational and scientific processes. Modern attitudes regard the past as outmoded or traditional. The original term used to describe pre-modern societies was "primitive" with all the negative connotations that carries. More recently, the term "traditional" has become preferred, and sociological attitudes toward the pre-modern past vary from still negative to what I consider almost romantic connotations, where past forms of organization are idealized in comparison with the chaotic present. Current views depict the present as a struggle or a transition toward a technological and sociopolitical better future. Society is not only the direct product of humans, but humans can also perfect it. Some theories see positive change as natural and inevitable; others as something requiring reform and even revolution. Yet, belief in the potential perfectibility of society remains constant. This progressive essence translates into our first distinctive goal. Sociologists believe that society can be improved, and that the application of sociological methods and theories can "positively" contribute to what the Founding Fathers envisioned as "a more perfect union." We would not spend so much time critically analyzing the social if we did not believe that something better could be created (Fuller, 2006).

The origins of Sociology are linked not only to aspirations of progress but to a search for truth. Early sociologists attempted to practice positive science, a value-neutral, empirically oriented effort to locate "truth." The word Sociology was coined in the mid-nineteenth century by Auguste Comte, who is considered a pioneer of the discipline along with Emile Durkheim, Karl Marx, and Max Weber. He envisioned Sociology as a positive science devoid of ideology.

Historical sociological analysis has shown what went wrong through our obsessions with progress and truth. History has demonstrated that there is no value-neutral science. Positivism is associated with a singular definition of progress and a single process to achieve it. In Western countries, that process is always defined and dominated by those with political and economic power. These notions inspired and spread ideologies of subordination that destroyed traditional ways of life in non-Western societies and marginalized the voices of minorities all over the world.

The concept of progress itself carries a bias favoring Western ideas of modernity and the assumption that all change is good and/or necessary.

Beyond the damage inflicted by sociological views of "progress," we sociologists can also be blamed for our role in the maintenance of an unjust status quo. While many sociologists have been part of progressive movements, still others have directly or indirectly supported institutions and organizations now shown to be racist, sexist, ethnocentric, and hosts to multiple sins. As a discipline, Sociology has spent the last 70 years analyzing and denouncing the systems of oppression that we formerly supported, either intentionally or inadvertently. We have learned to see progress as an inherently democratic and participatory process, devoting considerable time and energy to unmasking the instruments of oppression and amplifying the voices of underrepresented, underheard, and marginalized minorities.

Can we reconcile this history and still believe in Sociology's power as a positive force for society? Yes, because we have learned from our past and have changed accordingly. We have developed a more nuanced and complex view of progress. We can analyze the negative consequences of societies with an eye toward improving them if we recognize that those within the communities we study must have a voice in the definition of what "progress" would be for them. They should also have a role in how to accomplish such progress. We now know there is no one, ideal society; one person's utopia is someone else's dystopia. Social entities face multiple choices about what they want, each with different positive and negative consequences. The interests of the collective are not an excuse to ignore the dignity of individuals or their needs. This history provides the first five elements that form my own personal Statements of Goals and Values.

Given this history, sociologists should strive to adopt:

- A belief in the possibility of positive social change and the power of collective action;
- Emotional and intellectual openness to the needs and expectations of other people;
- The use of sociological knowledge to improve the lives of those around us, particularly marginalized populations;
- A spirit of collaboration and respect for the capacity of communities to define and contribute to their betterment;
- Value, appreciation, and respect for diversity in all its forms.

Behaviors to Avoid

For sociologists, what we stand *for* is as important as what we oppose. Our discipline sets the limits, then we develop theories and methods to provide us with insights about the issues and behaviors that Sociology majors should avoid. If you have taken Introduction to Sociology, you probably have heard or studied the sociological imagination, a concept created by C. Wright Mills (1959). At the core of the sociological imagination—our main form of asking questions and explaining society—is the assumption that the personal troubles of individuals can be explained through the lenses of social issues. Setting aside the "problem"-based nature of the sociological imagination, the core assumption holds that the quality of people's lives is directly related to the quality of the societies they inhabit. Better societies lead to better lives. Individualism, a philosophy that maintains that individuals pursuing their self-interest will benefit society the most, is the antithesis of sociological thinking. In the specific case of modern and postmodern societies, sociologists will also oppose individualism as a political philosophy. You would be hard-pressed to find a sociologist who thinks the United States would benefit from less social cohesion and coordination than current levels. As in the case of individualism, sociologists avoid the concept of freedom, believing it to be an illusion. We prefer to focus on agency: the capacity for action in the face of social constraints. A good society balances the interests and needs of the community with those of the individual, providing the right mix of structure and agency.

Social cohesion, the force that keeps communities together, is a central concept of Sociology. While it is generally considered a positive quality, sociological thinking cares about how it is achieved. Oppression, domination, and violence are clearly seen as negative forces. We study systems of domination (Gramsci & Hoare, 1971; Bourdieu, 1994) not only because they exist, but also because we believe that uncovering them can mitigate some of their effects. Better systems may provide individuals, if not with freedom, then at least with options for negotiated self-determination. In this spirit, sociologists must oppose the most egregious forms of domination and oppression, whether physical or cultural.

Let's consider the use of labels and their relationship to both violence and empowerment. It has long been established in Sociology that the use of labels to stigmatize groups is a form of symbolic violence (Goffman, 1963). Categorizing something as a disease, or abnormal, has a chilling effect and encourages greater suppression. Additionally, when applied to a group, labels can become one of the most insidious and underhanded forms of symbolic violence. Even apparently positive labels can be oppressive. For example, while many may think that referring to Americans of Asian descent as the "model minority" is positive, such a label has several negative consequences. It groups together communities that may not have anything in common, erasing their values and experiences. It obscures the specific challenges, particularly discrimination, that Asian Americans may have experienced or may still be suffering. It also can make this minority an unwilling participant in the domination over other groups. Labels unrelated to gender and race can also be used as a form of domination. Take the term "snowflake." The label implies fragility, but it is really an instrument to discount the opinions, needs, and emotions of a cohort generally relegated to positions of subordination to much older decision makers.

Sociologists must work hard to avoid:

- Individualism, both as a philosophy of action and as an explanation for behavior;
- Physical and symbolic violence in all its manifestations;
- Coercion in interactions among individuals and within social entities such as groups, organizations, institutions, and nations;
- Labels that erase or stigmatize people (but encourage the use of labels that empower);
- Language that hides or masks the true nature of social relationships, systems, processes, and issues.

Political Responsibilities

One of the main struggles in higher education comes from the tension between its civic and economic purposes. Central to this struggle is the premise that higher education should try to produce better people and better citizens. Equally valid is the notion that its chief purpose is to increase graduates' potential earning power. I am writing this book because I believe Sociology can do both. It can provide you with skills to enhance personal economic success and simultaneously enhance your knowledge of all the ways in which we can contribute to a better society.

Knowledge creates all sorts of responsibilities including perhaps the greatest: a vibrant political life. Sociologists are especially prepared to understand the value of the civic obligation of speaking truth to power. That extends to leaders in government and business. Economists are famous for ignoring what they call the problem of "externalities," the potential negative consequences of economic activity. In their view, private organizations are not responsible for the negative consequences of their production activities, and economists are not interested in studying them. Sociologists are different. These consequences *are* our concern; we tend to think that organizations should be accountable for the consequences of their actions.

Sociologists study and care both about the quantity and quality of jobs. A society that produces exploitative jobs has a lot of room for improvement. While sociologists who practice positive science may disagree, all sociologists, especially Sociology majors, can practice both science and activism, albeit perhaps not at the same time. We should recognize and denounce exploitation in all its forms and anything that diminishes human potential. We can demonstrate this commitment by supporting measures such as living wages, flexible work arrangements, family-friendly policies like paternity leave, and paid sick days. We may disagree on who should provide these benefits—the government or employers—but most sociologists are comfortable with the idea that they should be universally available. And while acknowledging that a potential loss in economic dynamism may follow, such loss can be a worthy sacrifice. The quality of life of families and workers is more important than the growth of Gross Domestic Product (GDP).

As sociologists we are aware of capitalism's potential as an economic system to create extreme inequality, threatening solidarity and cohesion within society (Marx & Engels, 1967). Sociologists would like to see a world with less inequality, certainly less than current twenty-first-century levels in the US. We may disagree about whether inequality is completely avoidable, or how much inequality is "necessary" to maintain a healthy division of labor that motivates people. We may differ about which dimensions of inequality need to be addressed or specific mechanisms for reducing it. But with levels of inequality increasing ever since the mid-1980s, and the myriad social problems associated with these higher levels confronting us, no sociologist is going to endorse greater inequality.

Sociologists are also likely to question the notion of "equality of opportunity" as the sole aspiration of societies. Professionals in other disciplines, particularly in the United States, are extremely comfortable with the accommodation of "merit"-based distribution of rewards through equality of opportunity. Sociologists know that equality of opportunity is impossible without equal distribution of other resources. Equality among unequals is not equality. Sociological theory also views merit as a social construct used to justify the privileges of elite groups (Bourdieu, 1984; Lamont, 1992; Mills, 1956). If people from certain groups must work twice as hard to be recognized as their more privileged peers, "merit" is at best an aspiration and at worst a sign of hypocrisy.

Does that mean that sociologists are "leftists?" Or communists? Since sociologists put communities at the center of life, we do not tend toward libertarianism as a political philosophy. But Sociology is an equal opportunity science, with all systems being the object of our analytical tools. Sociologists have directed much critical light on the problems associated with the forms of centralized (as in Russia) or decentralized (in China) authoritarian government as the main mechanism of resource distribution. Communist countries created their own unequal systems. Power and resources gravitated toward Party membership and political networks. Communism was unbelievably bad at creating wealth.

Many sociologists consider themselves part of the Marxist tradition, including me. Yet, few would recommend Communist regimes as the preferred form of government. The views of sociologists span the continuum from conservative to radical. Within that spectrum, theories focused more on social cohesion, the functionality of systems, and the role of tradition in society (Durkheim, 1972) can be regarded as "conservative" while those concentrating on "critical theories" (Foucault, 2007) tend to be characterized as "liberal," "radical," or "socialist." Keep in mind that these labels and their associations cannot encompass the diverse range of sociological thought. For example, a statist believes that government should have an active role in redistributing resources. Others prefer to confine the state to funding redistribution, limiting its job to providing money to nonprofits to deliver social goods and services. Some people favor community organizing and self-sustainability, linking the erosion of traditional community ties to inequality. Others see the voluntary reorientation of markets and organizations toward the social good as the only viable solution to our persisting social, economic, and political problems. Those who describe these different approaches as "socialist" may be proffering a stigmatizing label to support their political goals. Regardless of labels, anyone with sociological training has the obligation to engage in an active political life that takes into consideration the interests of marginalized people.

To fulfill their political responsibilities, sociologists must:

- Promote the accountability of political, economic, social leaders, and those who have power over others;
- Promote the redistribution of resources to mitigate the injustices of capitalism.

Economic Responsibilities

Political activism does not absolve sociologists from personal responsibilities when interacting with others. Ideally, we would like to see systemic changes reduce exploitation and alienation. We also should be aware of and try to minimize our own personal contributions to those conditions. Even with knowledge and good intentions, however, we too will inevitably play some part in systems of exploitation, domination, and oppression. As Sociology theory classes teach us, there is always an element of unwilling participation. Even sociologists who are hyperaware of the trappings of social systems cannot completely escape the "iron cage" formed by culture and society (Weber, 2002).

The freedom of thought potentially derived from critical thinking cannot liberate us from structural constraints. Under global capitalism, it is impossible to escape relationships of domination, in which the will and needs of some are imposed on others through a variety of means. The transfer of resources from poor to rich countries in the global economy (Wallerstein, 1979) is one such inescapable relationship. Even life in Sweden, the most socially oriented country in the world, doesn't preclude individuals from benefiting from the exploitation of workers in China, technically another socialist country. Minimum-wage workers in the US still benefit from the use of unregulated domestic farm labor through the availability of cheap processed food. Workers with retirement accounts benefit from the transfer of resources from other workers who created wealth. Even people who do urban scavenging to avoid consumerism are benefiting from the exploitation and alienation of others. They may avoid buying new goods themselves and collect society's leftovers (including food discarded by restaurants at the end of the day), but they really are not avoiding capitalism given that their scavenging is possible precisely because of capitalistic overproduction tendencies and the buying (and discarding) behaviors of consumers.

While sociologists should try to minimize their negative impact on others, they should also not feel guilty about not being perfect. Acknowledging that the institutions of capitalism are inescapable, individuals can make small but significant differences in the lives of others. I want to particularly emphasize our obligations to service workers. The demands placed on service workers by modern service standards in postmodern economies are dehumanizing. The demands of emotional labor are often unreasonable and the wages low. Our interdependence obligates us to be aware of their conditions, including their lack of autonomy and power. When interacting with service workers, a sociologist should avoid thinking or acting as if "the customer is always right." We should also be willing to pay higher prices for goods and services, as long as they are used to benefit workers rather than the bottom line of corporations.

It is impossible to avoid benefiting from the work of others. Interdependence is an inevitable consequence of living in society. Nor does our participation in civil action release us from our responsibility to others. Capitalism may obscure relationships of power, but it is our job to recognize them and provide "reparations." A sociologist should honor those relationships by contributing resources, both material and intellectual, to the causes of those less privileged than we are.

To fulfill our economic responsibilities, sociologists must:

- Treat workers in all industries and jobs with respect and dignity and support living wages for all;
- Support with money, labor, attention, or sponsorship those companies and organizations that produce positive social consequences; avoid supporting those creating negative ones.

Easy, no? Well, as a sociologist, you cannot expect improving society to be easy or to find the perfect strategy embodied in a single statement. Fourteen statements do not cover all the potential ways that Sociology tells us how to contribute to better societies. You may even directly oppose some of the statements that I have chosen for myself. Select the goals most central to you, both as a sociologist and as a person. Create new goals with your discoveries from Sociology classes, then prioritize them. Keep in mind that these goals are aspirational. Perfection is beyond the reach of us all. Don't let perfectionism become the enemy of effective action. The search for the best society is no different from the search for truth. It may well be impossible, but that's no excuse not to try.

Conclusion

Both in the classroom and in the practice of creating knowledge, Sociology faculty go to great lengths to emphasize the scientific components of our discipline. Systematic critical thinking is and should be an intrinsic part of the sociological identity for faculty, students, and graduates. The world would be a better place if everybody, not just sociologists, were able to recognize biases and taken-for-granted assumptions, and tried to minimize them when they arise. However, to achieve the sociological goal of making a better society, knowledge has to be transformed into actions. Normative elements are part of all scientific endeavors. Denying or obscuring them only diminishes the impact of the discipline in the world. Our capacity to bring sociologically informed ethics to the workplace, and to orient our behaviors to follow those ethics, is one important but unsung advantage that Sociology majors have over graduates of other disciplines. We should flaunt it, not hide it.

Discussion Questions

1. Think of your favorite sociological topic, researcher, or article. Is there a normative statement embedded within it that tells you how to behave in the future?
2. Think of your interactions with people of power (managers, teachers, parents). Have they behaved in a sociologically ethical way? How could they have behaved better?
3. Think of your interactions with service workers. How have you demonstrated sociologically enlightened ethical behavior? How can you improve your behavior?
4. Are there any specific organizations or industries that you think a sociologist should avoid because of ethical considerations?
5. Are there any specific jobs that you think sociologists should avoid because of ethical considerations?
6. What do you think are the most important ethical issues facing sociologists today?
7. Are your personal politics related to your sociological training? How?
8. In your opinion, are the normative and scientific elements of Sociology in opposition to each other? In other words, is a practical Sociology a less scientific one?
9. Can someone be conservative and still follow sociological ethics?
10. What are the biggest contemporary ethical issues not covered in this chapter?

Action/Reflection Activity

1. Create your own Statement of Values and Goals:
   (a) Read each goal listed in this chapter and extract those you believe are most important or applicable to your future career and way of life.
   (b) Modify those goals to make them personal and specific to your own career path.
   (c) Add other goals, issues, or values important to you from an ethical perspective.

Works Cited

Bourdieu, P. (1984). *Distinction: A social critique of the judgement of taste*. Harvard University Press.
Bourdieu, P. (1994). Stratégies de reproduction et modes de domination. *Actes de la Recherche en Sciences Sociales, 105*(1), 3–12.
Durkheim, E. (1893). *The division of labour in society*. New York.
Durkheim, E. (1972). *Emile Durkheim: Selected writings*. Cambridge University Press.
Foucault, M. (2007). *Discipline and punishment: The birth of the prison*. Duke University Press.
Fuller, S. (2006). *The new sociological imagination*. Sage.
Giddens, A. (1990). The Consequences of Modernity: Stanford University Press.
Goffman, E. (1963). *Stigma and social identity*. Prentice-Hall, Inc.
Gramsci, A., & Hoare, Q. (1971). *Selections from the prison notebooks*. Lawrence and Wishart.
Lamont, M. (1992). *Money, morals, manners*. University of Chicago Press.
Marx, K., & Engels, F. (1967). *The communist manifesto (1848)* (S. Moore, Trans.). Penguin.
Wallerstein, I. (1979). *The capitalist world-economy*. Cambridge University Press.
Weber, M. (2002). *The Protestant ethic and the "spirit" of capitalism and other writings*. Penguin.
Mills, C. W. (1956). 72 *The Power Elite*. In Inequality Classic Readings in Race, Class, and Gender. Routledge, 71–86.
Mills, C. W. (1959). *The sociological imagination*. Oxford University Press.
Zeitlin, I. M. (2001). *Ideology and the development of sociological theory*. Pearson College Division.

Community Building for Sociologists 4

The sociological professional identity offers a way of thinking but no direct path to guide your actions or career. Chapters 2 and 3 provided ideas and frameworks for the ongoing task of developing and maintaining an identity of your own. I will now turn to some practical ways for you to expand the scope of your work of identity formation through two tasks not explicitly covered in most Sociology curriculums: community creation and career networking.

As we grow older, community becomes less a given and more an act of self-authoring. We must consciously decide who we want to become. You had little choice about the community your parents and school created for you before you went to college. In the transition from high school to college, you are presented with opportunities to create a community of like-minded people, starting with your professors and classmates. A variety of events, student groups, and other extracurricular activities offer additional opportunities to build new communities, both professional and personal.

The task of community creation in college is intimately related to the development of your identity(ies), professional or otherwise. We often discover and develop who we are through the people we encounter. Sometimes that includes deciding who we are *not*, by being exposed to people with whom we disagree. The university opens the world to students, both its positive and dark sides, within a safe environment. Given how segregated America is, that may include your first encounter with individuals from different racial, ethnic, and socioeconomic backgrounds than yours. Most colleges also provide a variety of opportunities to study abroad or to interact with faculty or students from different countries. You will never again have such a wealth of resources available in one place to expand your

© The Author(s), under exclusive license to Springer Nature Switzerland AG 2023
M. A. Martinez, *The Employable Sociologist*,
https://doi.org/10.1007/978-3-031-41323-0_4

world and construct a cosmopolitan and rich identity. The world is vast and full of wonders; use this opportunity to explore it.

College students can have a variety of experiences in America. Some are studying in an Ivy League institution or a top-tier university where you are pushed into an immersive college experience that makes the university your whole life. Others are studying in a commuter school or have to work full- or part-time to pay for your studies. Whatever your circumstances, you should do your best to invest time or money—your most valuable resources—into investigating and utilizing the opportunities presented to you. If money is an issue, there are options like work-study, paid internships, and study abroad scholarships. Investing a little bit of time in talking to your advisor, professors, classmates, and university departments can give you a big pay-off in resources and experiences.

I have heard many Sociology alumni and faculty talk about job searching as the process of "finding your tribe." They recommend making sure that you like the people who will be your co-workers. Your own goals, however, may take you in a different direction. Consider my example. I could have stayed in Mexico, got a job as a Communication major, or even become a professor in that field. Instead, I transplanted myself, alone, to a different country. I also selected a connected but significantly different area of study. My own motivation was less about finding my tribe than finding a space where I could be myself even if not necessarily among others like me. I was looking for control over my own life, personally and intellectually. And if I am honest, I wanted some prestige and power. Those decisions about who I wanted to be and what elements I valued in a community determined my path.

In addition to creating your community, you also should develop mechanisms that allow you to keep your community after graduation. As a sociologist, once you leave school you will work in environments where individuals will have different educational experiences than yours. A department or an organization is not likely to be composed exclusively or even mainly by sociologists. In some situations, you may be a "token" (Kanter, 2008) sociologist in a group where other types of majors are more common. You can still find community and learn about yourself amidst an environment where you provide intellectual diversity. I found Sociology and my place within it in the most unexpected place: a Business School. While I was bouncing from one communication-related job to another, a former professor offered me a job as an advisor for the Business School at my alma mater. At that point, a stable salary and good benefits sounded like paradise. Because free education was one of the benefits, I took a couple MBA classes, talked with Business faculty about their work, and helped students make their classes work for them. While I discovered I did not want to be a manager, I thought managers were a fascinating object of study. My short involvement in the world of management has provided me with inspiration and materials for this book.

You also need to "network" to explore and develop new relationships that may guide you toward a future career. The difference between creating community and networking is that while communities may provide resources for career development, relationships are based more on emotional (expressive) elements. Communities provide emotional support and are a strong component of your identity. Networks tend to be more instrumental—important for the resources they let you access. While everybody in your community will be part of your network, not everybody in your network will have a significant role in your life. The process of creating community is similar to that of networking. However, because the type of relationships and their goals are different, I have separated and will take up networking in the next chapter. This one is designed to help you understand some of the principles of community creation and their consequences while providing you with strategies to "find your tribe."

Nature of Social Relationships

Sometimes our natural tendencies will help us create better relationships. Other times they will be an obstacle to our community-building goals. While a few pages cannot do justice to the topic of social relationships and their characteristics, there are some key principles to keep in mind when you engage in the work of community building. The tendencies and principles we will explore are homophily, reciprocity, role fit, and privacy.

Homophily

Sociology defines homophily as the general tendency to make connections with people who are like us. Part of our evolution as social beings is distinguishing between those who are like "us" versus those who are "other." Homophilia does not mean that everybody in a group or community is equal. Some people "belong" in a group more than others. The level of belonging is the product of contested negotiations among members. There is always conflict about which members represent or embody the essence of a group versus which ones are almost outsiders.

Bounded solidarity, a concept developed by Sensenbrenner and Portes (2018), explains that homophily, as well as other characteristics such as social cohesion, is stronger when particular groups have shared experiences of discrimination and struggle. Bounded solidarity normally reinforces homogenous communities along racial and ethnic lines.

Centrality in a community represents power and prestige. Being at the outside border of a community is a more ambiguous position. While it may make individuals targets of discrimination and aggressive behavior, it also puts them in the unique position to connect with other groups and communities. Such external connections can transform into opportunities both for the individual and their group. In Chap. 2 we talked about how faculty define undergraduates as ambassadors of Sociology, placing you in the outside boundary of the discipline. That position can have negative consequences, such as some faculty's ignoring of your career development needs. But it also offers opportunities that faculty seldom reach.

Belonging to homogenous communities provides readily available expressive rewards. It helps us reinforce and solidify a positive identity. We avoid diverse relationships and communities for the opposite reasons. From a sociopsychological perspective, crossing any social boundary creates anxiety. The anxiety is greater when the borders are created by social categories like gender, race, ethnicity, and class. One would imagine that in the US, given the cultural emphasis on egalitarianism, class boundaries would not exist. Yet, people feel very anxious when talking to those with more power or prestige than themselves. Crossing gender and race boundaries also creates anxiety, fears of causing offense or feeling awkward. The problem of homophily is never quite separate from that of status. We favor relationships with people of our same status. Gender, race, ethnicity, and class are identity-based boundaries, but they are also systems of categorizing by hierarchical status. Anxiety about crossing one of these boundaries can also be about inadvertently causing offense to members of already discriminated and marginalized groups. Interaction mistakes under these conditions may be interpreted as microaggressions.

While it is natural to find satisfaction and comfort in homogenous communities, sociologists have an obligation to resist this tendency. If we endorse the idea that diverse communities are a positive development in social evolution, then we must engage in and promote diverse contacts ourselves. Forcing ourselves to engage in diverse networking is a first step toward promoting diverse societies. Getting to know diverse people is a pre-condition for creating diverse communities.

Hybrid Nature

Sociology describes community relationships as expressive or emotional and professional networks as more instrumental. In reality, almost all relationships are a mix of the two components (Lin, 2002). Expressive elements reflect the affective components enmeshed in a relationship. We consider love, for example, in its many forms, including attraction, liking, or admiration. Sometimes competition or even hatred can be an expressive tie, as in the case of frenemies.

Instrumental elements refer to the interdependence between roles in society, what Durkheim called organic solidarity (1893). We normally think of instrumental relationships in terms of economics; the division of labor in society allows us to efficiently produce and exchange necessary goods and services. Other people have resources, money, or information that we need to survive.

Certain contexts require a specific combination of expressive and instrumental elements in relationships. For example, "parent" is supposed to have a stronger expressive component while "boss" is more instrumental. No role is completely pure; parents fulfill the needs of their children by providing food and shelter. Even later in life, when societal expectations assume that adult children will be financially and socially independent, parents still often contribute money or babysitting time. There is a general assumption that instrumental relationships should govern our careers and that expressive ones dominate our personal lives. Professionalization (not to be confused with belonging to a profession) includes the process of separating the public from the private, the personal from the "office." While this separation is viewed as an ideal, we all fail to fulfill it. Because of our intensive and extensive interactions with bosses, subordinates, and colleagues, we tend to find friends and even romantic partners among them. Sometimes the organization itself supports the creation of expressive ties. Companies have discovered that productivity is improved by developing or simulating an expressive component inside the organization. After all, there is no more perfect mechanism from which to extract free labor than families (Portes, 1998). Finding the right balance of instrumental and expressive relationships in the workplace is a matter of much individual and social debate.

Reciprocity

Both instrumental and expressive components of relationships are more satisfactory when there is reciprocity among the parties involved (Gouldner, 1960). That means that the exchange of benefits, either of an emotional or economic nature, should be equal. The expectation of equality is truly clear in how we think about modern marriages. My husband always says to me, usually when we are discussing the division of household labor, that marriage is not a calculation about equality. However, as a sociologist, I must respond that it sort of is. An informal rule in all relationships is that they must be (somewhat) equally beneficial. Reciprocity may not necessarily be about exchanging the same benefit (i.e., money, advice, time); in marriages organized around specialized division of labor, one partner concentrates on making money on the labor market while the other focuses on household management. The benefits can also shift at different times. Continuing the example about marriage, one partner may stay at home for several years to raise the couple's children while the other concentrates on their career, and later they exchange roles to provide a sense of long-term equality of opportunity.

Regardless of the timing, healthy relationships are assumed to be reciprocal. Relationships that are unequal by nature tend to be seen as problematic. That may help explain your own reluctance to develop relationships with those who can help you develop your career. As a student or recent graduate trying to start your career, you are in a vulnerable position. You may feel that networking unfairly imposes upon others; you need their help more than they need yours. Your repayment of any kind of assistance looks uncertain and far in the future. In this sense, status is not only a social barrier, but a proxy for potential reciprocity.

Public Separation

As a first-generation immigrant to the US, I am constantly surprised by how central privacy and autonomy are to American culture. Individuals are entitled to a lot of control concerning what information about themselves they share in social interactions. This control varies dramatically. Some people, for example, overshare on social media; others keep the details of their lives completely to themselves. As a consequence, it becomes difficult to predict levels of sharing that are implied in particular relations, so it is safer just not to share. By making autonomy and control a priority, we create invisible barriers to community.

For a particular social category, that of the "stranger," most people assume that there is no obligation to share anything, not even small talk. Experimental psychologists Juliana Schroeder and Nicholas Eppley's work on interactions among strangers shows that we tend to overestimate other people's desire for solitude and underestimate the pleasure that we and others feel during those conversations. When we are in the middle of such interactions, we find them more satisfactory than we initially expected (Schroeder et al., 2022). Their experiments took place on commuter trains, a setting where we make an art of avoiding talking to each other or making eye contact. It is unlikely that you will be engaged in career development networking during your commute (although you never know). As students new to relationship building, interactions with strangers even in settings designed for that purpose approaching strangers may feel like a violation of other people's privacy and a waste of their time. Excessive concern for personal boundaries and fear of transgressing them are real obstacles to community building. To create community, you must "put yourself out there."

Homophily, rules of reciprocity, ambiguity between expressive and instrumental relationship components, and high levels of assumed public separation are all direct obstacles that you will have to overcome to create a diverse and strong career community. To overcome them, you will have to cross traditional social boundaries and interact with people.

Frames to Fight Anxiety

While there is no magic recipe to avoid anxiety during social interactions, you may find it useful to keep in mind the points that follow.

Community Building and Networking Are Part of Any Job Managerial science clearly demonstrates that relationship building and networking are part of the daily work in many organizational positions. For positions requiring a college degree, the social component of the job is more central. Conferences, career fairs, cocktail hours, and similar group events are specifically designed to help train you in developing this important job function. All participants share this obligation. When you network with people, you help them perform their jobs. Experienced people go to events to achieve their own personal goals. Even the most prestigious speaker attends a conference to see what other people are doing and exchange ideas. Every person representing an employer in a career fair is there because their job is to promote their organization and find potential recruits. Neither they nor you can predict if that relationship will pay off, but that is an accepted part of the interaction. You may find the occasional grumpy participant, but if they rebuff your efforts, they are the ones not doing their job.

Of course, our emotional reactions are often not rational. Feeling anxious when interacting with strangers is normal. The last few years of the COVID pandemic and political strife have not helped. Chapter 5, on networking, includes tools to create scripts to help you prepare for interactions in advance. Another way to alleviate these feelings is to concentrate on participants' common goals and the potential for positive outcomes. People attend networking events because they are valuable to themselves personally and to their organizations. Like you, they do not know what opportunities may arise from the interactions. Everybody is in the same boat. Yes, awkwardness may be a part of the interaction, but the potential rewards they may hold for both your career and your mental health are worth some discomfort.

Crossing Social Boundaries Supports Social Justice The propensity to cross social boundaries for networking and community development is not equally distributed in society. People from privileged and powerful groups are more likely to feel entitled to cross those boundaries. For an excellent article on how cognitive biases differ in people of higher status, I recommend "Cognition in a Hierarchy" by Ricardo Blaug (2007). If you are a student from an underprivileged background, learning to cross social boundaries is a tool to balance the injustices of modern societies. If you are a student from a privileged socioeconomic background or a graduate of an Ivy League university, you have an opportunity to respectfully, humbly, and positively make yourself available to others. For everybody else, respectfully opening up ourselves to diverse communities and networks is part of our obligation to each other as human beings.

Reciprocity Is a Long-Term Proposition Despite how daunting the transition from school to work may seem and how unprepared you may feel right now, you will find your way. Most of us eventually land in satisfying and rewarding jobs. Once your career matures, you will be in a better position to help others. You may not be able to repay it directly through relationship reciprocity, but eventually you will be able to pay it forward. While reciprocity "calculations" are a part of all social interactions, modern societies tend to emphasize shorter horizons and a quantification of exchanges. Social exchanges are and should be more flexible than those in the market.

Strategies for "Finding Your Tribe"

Get to Know Your Professors Your classes provide a unique opportunity to get to know your professors, their expertise, and their trajectories. While some classes may provide a fantastic opportunity for community building, many do not. The professor's priorities are to fulfill the objectives of the class and give all students an opportunity to participate. I strongly encourage you to take advantage of office hours or make a personal appointment to talk to your professors outside the classroom setting. Similarly, you may want to review your department's website to explore the whole list of Sociology faculty, their biographies, writings, and research interests. Approach faculty who appear interesting to you.

There are many reasons why faculty do not teach classes related to their personal work, from enrollment issues to the need to cover other courses. Most faculty will be willing to help you with an independent study project if it fits within their area of interest and they are not planning to teach a class on that topic. Consider asking faculty about their connections to outside organizations, other departments and faculty who may interest you, events they recommend, or any of many other topics you could discuss. Develop close relationships with at least two faculty members who can write good recommendation letters for you and become references now or after graduation.

Research Your University One of the advantages of Sociology as a major is how compatible and complementary it is with many other areas of study. Depending on the structure of your degree, you may have varying opportunities to explore other areas of knowledge. Use whatever opportunities you are given to explore your identity and build your community. Reviewing other majors and minors offered by your university is the first step. Majors and minors can be thematic, that is, examining a topic from different perspectives. I have found that Sociology students get attracted to thematic majors or minors around social problems like immigration, food availability, and environmental issues. Other popular areas of study might include those associated with the experiences of groups such as Latinx, Black, Asian, or LGBTQ+. Majors and minors can also be skill-based. Sociology students might be attracted to topics like Human Resources, Social Marketing, Journalism, or even Graphic Design. You do not necessarily need to complete a double major or minor, but you can use the information to locate classes and faculty to enrich your community. I have seen students in their senior year finally discover a class or a faculty member who really reflected their interests and realize too late what they potentially lost. Also explore the different centers and departments within your university and keep an eye out for volunteer, internship, and job opportunities that interest you. In my experience, Sociology students have found opportunities in departments like Admissions, Student Affairs, Counseling, and many others.

Explore Your Family Relations For most of us, working for our family or a friend of the family is not a viable or appealing option. However, that does not mean your family has nothing to offer you in terms of potential mentors and contacts. Every adult in your life has their own communities. They may have developed these contacts through their school years, their jobs, and the organizations they have joined over their lives, including through church, sports clubs, and hobbies. Your relatives' connections can provide you with unexpected community and networking opportunities. Talk to your family about their life experiences and the people they have met along the way. That can bring you closer to your family and also expand your prospects for community.

Review Alumni Lists and Pages Sociology undergraduates can work in any industry or type of organization, and in a variety of departments and positions within them. Finding what Sociology alumni are doing can help you focus on specific choices. Most universities provide mechanisms to contact alumni mentors who volunteer to help students with informational interviews and other career development tasks. Some departments and universities may have alumni-related social media accounts that can provide you with career information on their former Sociology majors. While not all faculty keep social media accounts or make them accessible to students, you should also try to join those that do. Sharing with professors across time can be an excellent point of connection and a source of information about your potential career.

Stay Connected with College Friends No matter how busy you are with your studies, make sure you reserve some time for building relationships. You can combine your academic work with time with friends by organizing study groups or attending events with them. You should also create an electronic infrastructure or exchange information that will allow you to follow up with your college friends after graduation. As your life after college progresses, people will change and move. However, you will always share the challenges of being sociologists in the world. Some of my friends have ended up all over the globe and others stayed at home; I personally remade my area of study and practice, exchanging Communication for Sociology. Despite these "distances," my college friends know me in a way that my current community does not, and they remain a valuable source of emotional and social support. Some of you will be lucky enough to work in organizations with similar-minded people, but you may not. Never underestimate the importance of having a group of like-minded people supporting each other.

Develop Industry Connections I do not recommend that undergraduate students become members of the American Sociological Association unless you plan to study Sociology in graduate school to become a researcher or teacher. Membership is expensive and the association does not offer many services to undergraduates. If you already have a particular industry or sector in mind, you should periodically review trade magazines or newsletters in that area. Some trade magazines require subscriptions, but normally your university library can provide free access. If you have a specific position or department in mind, you may want to read or follow publications related to those areas. Table 4.1 offers examples of trade publications and newsletters in the nonprofit sector and Table 4.2 offers a similar list for social media. You can easily search online for trade publications in areas like education, housing, environmental issues, art, and museums. Similarly, try to identify key organizations that you admire or that you value for some reason. I recommend reviewing national and local lists of socially responsible organizations, organizations considered the best to work for, and industry leaders. Finally, as you come closer to graduation, consider formally becoming a member of professional or network associations at the national and local level. These memberships not only offer valuable information, but you can include them on your resume; membership helps prove both passion and expertise in the area.

Feed the Geek This is my advice not only for networking but for life. Because you can find Sociology everywhere, all your passions are connected to your sociological imagination and can feed the sociologist in you. As you graduate and leave educational institutions, you want your world to expand, not contract. Make sure you take time to follow your passions even if they are not related to your job. Continue to engage with the world sociologically, beyond and above the opportunities and limitations of whatever job you have at any particular time. It may be a

Table 4.1 Nonprofit trade publications

Nonprofit Trade Publications	
Nonprofit Quarterly	Alliance Magazine (Philanthropy and Social Investment)
Nonprofit PRO	Nonprofit Management & Leadership
The Nonprofit Times	Stanford Social Innovation Review
NYN Media	Journal of Philanthropy and Marketing
Journal of Public and Nonprofit Affairs	Voluntas

Table 4.2 Social media publications

Social Media Publications	
The Social Media Monthly	HOW (Design Magazine)
Social Media Today	Adweek
Social Media Examiner	AdAge
Social Media Magazine	The Drum
Social Media + Society	PR Week

cliché to say that the world is constantly changing, but it is true. Keep current in terms of scientific, market, organizational, and industry knowledge. Be aware of new industries, organizations, jobs, and job titles. Follow the trajectories in social media and elsewhere of people you admire. They can offer a source of inspiration amidst the mundane realities of a job.

Develop a Reflective Practice Relationship and community building is a valuable component in the process of creating your own professional identity, one that requires active reflection. We can all get too busy *doing* without giving ourselves enough time to process what we experience. Keeping a diary of your professional self is an effective form of reflection. You also may want to keep information about events and people to possibly use in the future. If you are an avid writer, a traditional diary format is good. For myself, using a form ensures that I will include the relevant information. Figure 4.1 is one example. Create whatever form fills your needs.

PROFESSIONAL REFLECTIVE JOURNAL

Event

Date

Participant Names /
Contact Information

Topic Summary

What I Learned About
Myself

Opportunities Detected

Follow-Up Actions

Fig. 4.1 Professional reflective journal

Conclusion

Building relationships and creating community(ies) is an integral part of the process of identity formation. Belonging to a Sociology undergraduate program provides you with the start of a community; one aspect of your professional development is to become an active relationship and community builder. Different departments in the university can offer you opportunities to practice relationship building while expanding your career horizons. "Finding your tribe" also helps you mold who you are and who you want to be as a professional. Understanding certain principles of social relationships, including homophily, hybrid expressive/instrumental elements, reciprocity, and public separation can help guide your relationship building efforts. Creating diverse communities can produce anxiety over crossing gender, racial, class, and ethnic borders. The ambiguity inherent in finding the right combination of expressive/instrumental dimensions for specific roles also induces anxiety. Framing relationship building efforts as a necessary part of both social justice and job performance can help alleviate these fears. Adopting a long-term view of reciprocity can offer further relief. To sum up, keep in mind these strategies for building relationships and creating community:

- Get to know your professors;
- Research the opportunities available within your university;
- Explore family connections;
- Review alumni lists and pages;
- Develop industry connections;
- Stay connected to college friends;
- Feed the geek;
- Develop a reflective practice.

Discussion Questions

1. Thinking of your current community, are you comfortable with its diversity?
2. Do you feel emotionally and intellectually supported?
3. Do you feel intellectually challenged?
4. Thinking of modern society, do you see an increased or decreased tendency toward homophily compared with the past? What are the advantages and disadvantages of current levels of homophily?

5. Thinking of your ideal future relationship with your boss, co-workers, and subordinates, what balance of expressive/instrumental elements should you personally aim for and why? Express it as percentages.
6. When was the last time you interacted with a stranger in an unstructured setting? How would you evaluate your interaction?
7. Thinking of your favorite and least favorite professors, describe your relationship with them in terms of homophily, reciprocity, and expressive/instrumental elements. Can you find in these concepts reasons for your preference?
8. On a scale from 1 to 10, assess your current level of anxiety/discomfort at relationship building. Can this chapter help you locate the sources of that anxiety? Are there other reasons?
9. Think of at least three strategies to reduce your anxiety over relationship building.
10. Can you think of two professors who would write a recommendation letter for you? Do they know the "real" you? What can you do to improve your chances of getting good recommendations?

Action/Reflection Activity

1. Relationship building:
    (a) Review the list and bios of faculty members in your Sociology Department. Select one or two and review their recent work.
    (b) Make an appointment with a faculty member to talk about your career development. Prepare a list of questions in advance.
    (c) Make an appointment with a Career Center advisor in your area of interest. Talk about where you are in your career journey and ask for next steps.
    (d) Locate a source of alumni information and review 20 individuals. Determine whether they might potentially offer you ideas on potential careers or career paths. If so, arrange for an informational interview. A template for informational interviews will be discussed in the next chapter.
    (e) Are there any sectors or industries that appeal to you? Choose one, then subscribe to one of their trade publications, newsletters, or podcasts. Continue to either follow that industry or research new ones that pique your interest.
    (f) Talk to your parents and friends about *their* friends and relatives. Do they have a contact who could potentially help you in your career?
    (g) Think of your closest five friends at school. Talk to them about the job you want and ask if they have some suggestions for you.

Works Cited

2. Reflection:
   (a) Design your own professional reflective journal.
   (b) Use it to record your Part I activities.

Works Cited

Blaug, R. (2007). Cognition in a hierarchy. *Contemporary Political Theory*, 6(1), 24–44.
Durkheim, E. (1893). *Division of labour*. Alcan.
Gouldner, A. W. (1960). The norm of reciprocity: A preliminary statement. *American Sociological Review*, 25(2), 161–178.
Kanter, R. M. (2008). *Men and women of the corporation* (New edition). Basic Books.
Lin, N. (2002). *Social capital: A theory of social structure and action* (Vol. 19). Cambridge University Press.
Portes, A. (1998). Social capital: Its origins and applications in modern sociology. *Annual Review of Sociology*, 24(1), 1–24.
Schroeder, J., Lyons, D., & Epley, N. (2022). Hello, stranger? Pleasant conversations are preceded by concerns about starting one. *Journal of Experimental Psychology: General*, 151(5), 1141.
Sensenbrenner, J., & Portes, A. (2018). Embeddedness and immigration: Notes on the social determinants of economic action. In *The sociology of economic life* (pp. 93–115). Routledge.

Networking for Sociologists 5

This book is predicated on the idea that Sociology offers values and skills that can enable you to achieve most of your professional and personal goals. Recontextualizing both your values and skills to approach the labor market will increase your chances of professional and personal success. In this chapter I address the reality that sometimes *who* you know may be as important as *what* you know. For a clear example where connections matter, take Ivanka Trump. Through her association with her father, she created a successful career in real estate. She also managed to walk the corridors of power and get access to some of the most influential people on the planet. When accused of benefiting from nepotism, she once said that while her father opened doors for her, she had to be competent enough to go through them. She may not recognize it, but finding and opening doors is one of the most difficult tasks in any career.

Ivanka Trump may not be the best example to offer Sociology students. Her opportunities come from inherited networks and privilege. You are unlikely to have a similar advantage. However, it is possible for you too to actively create networks that can help you in your career. The best example of a natural networker who has not relied on parental networks is Barack Obama. While he was obviously knowledgeable and deeply immersed in politics, each of his experiences also brought him an impressive array of contacts within Black communities, Hollywood, and the legal establishment. Even his selection of a wife, Michelle Obama, became a boon to his political career. He is also credited with being the first effective user of social media for campaign networking. As a Sociology student aware of the world around you, you can offer your own examples in which knowing the right person makes a difference in a career. Networking experience also can help you adapt and transform your career goals. You cannot aspire to a job you do not know exists, and the market is constantly creating new jobs or changing their titles.

Networking is more than just a strategy of career development and social mobility: it is a fundamental part of most jobs. Goals and functions in modern organizations are so complex that bureaucratic structures fail to achieve them. Reaching out to people across bureaucratic or departmental divides is fundamental. Organizations try to mimic the effects of networks by developing structures such as task forces or project-oriented networks of collaboration to handle issues like marketing or quality management (Manley, 2000). While task forces are only used in moments of crisis or for substantial projects, informal networks help bureaucracies regularly be more efficient and responsive (Heckscher, 1994). Networks are also important for interorganizational collaboration. Given how neoliberalism has pushed many organizations to outsource some functions, interorganizational networks have become critical. This is particularly the case in areas that may interest you, like health care and social services (Gittell & Weiss, 2004).

The design and practice of network strategies is a fundamental part of any professional identity. If you are anything like my Sociology students, you have not started serious networking efforts. If pushed to say why not, students usually say they do not know how to begin. Despite the efforts of universities and Sociology Departments to provide opportunities to get to know professionals and organizations in many fields, if you are like my students you have let those opportunities pass. Your professors also err in thinking that if the university offers opportunities, students will automatically take advantage of them. This is an area in which you may be at a disadvantage compared to other majors like Business, which push participation in networking efforts from the first year of college. This chapter is dedicated to understanding networking, the obstacles that Sociology students face, and how to overcome them.

Hopefully, this knowledge will convince you to take control of your networking efforts. I begin by summarizing what Sociology knows about networking and its impact on career success. Then I explore sociological explanations for the anxiety and guilt so often associated with networking, and discuss guilt about privilege and a lack of scripts to guide behavior. That eads to a consideration of strategies to deal with the anxiety, concluding with suggestions on how to identify and approach contacts.

The Sociology of Networks

The irony of this networking problem is that Sociology has deeply studied the subject both inside and outside professional environments. The first sociological study of networking in the context of the labor market was done by Granovetter in 1973. His work is based on the idea that to get good jobs, people need to know that those jobs exist. He hypothesized that relationships with high homophily (where individuals are similar to each other) offered less opportunities to find the best jobs than those with more diverse contacts. People with diverse contacts had access to information beyond their own immediate environments (Granovetter, 1973) that could help them achieve social mobility. A broader concept, called social capital, was developed to highlight the benefits of informal social structures. Social capital identifies benefits in both close and diverse networks, depending on the resources required. Burt (2018) continues the analysis of the economic advantages of diverse ties, introducing the concept of structural holes. Diverse ties usually bridge the "holes" between social groups, providing unique and more valuable opportunities to make money. Coleman used these ideas to describe the positive effect of cohesion, defined as belonging to strong and closed networks, in children's educational achievement (Coleman, 1988). Social capital as cohesion has also been used to explain the work of family businesses in communities of immigrants across the world (Sensenbrenner & Portes, 2018) and how elites provide preferential access and hoard opportunities for their members even within supposedly merit-based societies (Coleman, 1988). Networks and social capital that bridge different departments and divisions also provide performance advantages for both organizations and those who are part of their internal labor markets (Burt, 2000). Diverse networks allow workers to identify and skirt bureaucratic hoops and coordinate complex tasks, which results in better performances for individuals and better outcomes for the organization (Burt et al., 2000). While most organizations insist on open job searches, applicants with internal networks and recommendations have a positive advantage during the selection process. The literature on community development integrates both concepts of bridging (diverse) and bonding (cohesive) social capital to facilitate economic development in underdeveloped areas of the world (Woolcock & Narayan, 2000). Perhaps the most famous application of the idea of social capital outside Sociology was Robert Putnam's book, Bowling Alone (2000). As a political scientist, he attributes the decline of American democracy and civil society to the decline of public participation in informal groups, including sports leagues, volunteer activities, and even dinner nights among friends.

The literature on social capital peaked in the early 2000s. Although it is still applied broadly in specific contexts, new theoretical developments and transformational empirical studies in this area have been rare. The reason for this decline is that despite its potential for helping individuals, social capital and its effects are distributed across dimensions similar to those found in other resources in society. Networks have difficulty crossing race, gender, and class lines. This means, for example, that women in general tend to create the kind of networks that fail to help them succeed in the organizational environment, just as gender itself disadvantages women (Cross & Lin, 2008). Similar dynamics appear in the areas of race, ethnicity, and class (Pichler & Wallace, 2009).

Networks and social capital should be developed and utilized so that they are available to you when the opportunity arises. Two characteristics complicate the use of social capital. First, the usefulness of social capital depends on the situation (Burt, 2009). While contingency can be applied to all the possible ways in which people can help you, Burt was referring to labor market conditions. He found that given a variety of equally qualified candidates for a position, social capital becomes a way to gain an advantage, as demonstrated when an employer chooses an already existing employee for the job. This phenomenon also may be at play in early selection procedures where even if a computer discards your application in the first round, an email from an internal source can get you back in the game. Contacts and relationships with any stakeholder in the organization (employees, consumers, community, watchdog groups, trade associations, etc.) are an advantage in the selection process. Those relationships are evidence of communication and teamwork skills, which the organization can use to help it achieve its goals.

Cultural differences determine the appropriateness of using these expressive social connections to achieve personal goals. For example, while blatant cases of nepotism are judged badly in the West, the phenomenon is called guanxi in China and is considered an accepted social practice. There are also class variations: rich people and members of elites feel more comfortable using their connections than those with less economic resources.

Internet-Based Networking

Much like the printing press, the Internet was once seen as a technology capable of fundamentally modifying the very nature of how humans related to each other. People believed it would provide an opportunity to increase the democratization of both political systems and civic culture(s). The effect was supposed to happen in undemocratic places (such as China, Russia, North Korea) as well as in Western democracies (Dahlgren, 2000). It was also supposed to lead to more egalitarian social relationships less affected by racial, class, and gender differences (DiMaggio et al., 2001). Providing access to the Internet was also seen as having the potential to create equality of educational opportunity. It enables inexpensive and convenient communication with far-flung communities of shared interests.

Initial optimism about the Internet's potential has been replaced since by more apocalyptic predictions. It is beyond the scope of this chapter to evaluate the social impact of the Internet, but for career development the Internet makes it easy to find information about jobs, organizations, salaries, benefits, organizational culture, and a myriad of job-related topics. However, it can also lead to information overload. Deciding how and where (within the metaverse) to start your networking activities can be difficult.

While the Internet's informational benefits are real, it does not replace the role of networking in your job search. Professional contacts, diverse or not, continue to be key. While electronic announcements and application forms make it easier than ever to apply for a job, you now face more competition for the same positions. The greater the number of applications, the more mechanical the preliminary selection process becomes. Human Resources professionals may apply even more random and minor criteria to reduce the initial number of applications. Computer algorithms may also automatically eliminate applicants in ways that are difficult to predict and may be unintentionally discriminatory. From this perspective, the Internet has eliminated social capital's geographical limitation. Readily available email information allows applicants to make contacts all over the world. The pandemic brought its own networking boom with the pervasive use of Zoom for informational interviews and other types of personal or semi-personal contacts. At the same time, we are starting to discover that electronically created social capital operates much like it does in person. For example, researchers analyzing LinkedIn data on job searchers found that getting a job was positively correlated with the presence of weak ties (Rajkumar et al., 2022). Like Granovetter's findings of 1973, they concluded that networks containing a combination of both weak and strong ties are better at helping people find good jobs.

While the Internet increases your networking potential, it also presents you with the task of developing and enacting your social capital. That process entails subscribing to the right service platforms or networks; creating attractive and effective profiles and content; linking to interesting people, and devoting time to reading articles and messages. You may even have to switch applications or platforms as innovations appear or platforms gain or lose popularity. And don't ignore issues of privacy. Effective networking requires disclosing some details of your professional and personal life. Everything you post on those platforms is at risk of becoming public. Other concerns are a potential increase in your spam or the hazard of spending more time networking than working or living. In extreme cases, you may encounter active or passive stalking. These issues are real. Depending on the platform or the app, good social media training will give you ways to minimize risk. However, you will not be able to eliminate it completely. Electronic recruitment and selection may ebb and flow in popularity, but they will not disappear. Limiting your online presence and networking activities will lose you some opportunities. The decision to pay this price depends solely on you.

Guilt and the Myth of Meritocracy

Yet, despite the amount of events and mechanisms for networking offered by universities and the Internet's potential to open the world to people, Sociology undergraduates tend to avoid networking situations. There are two reasons for this reluctance: guilt and anxiety. My students say that networking just does not "feel right" to them. They see it as somewhat "inauthentic" and "unfair," something fundamentally wrong. One potential reason is our persistent internalization of merit as a fundamental value. Yet, Sociology has long established that our societies are not meritocratic. Sociological studies of stratification document that wealth, education, income, and other resources are not distributed equally across groups. We also know that such inequality is highly associated with inherited or ascriptive elements like gender, race, and parental educational and occupational background. It is beyond the scope of this book to describe all the intersectional and cumulative inequalities regarding life and career outcomes, but for more information, I recommend works by Savage (2021), Pfeffer and Killewald (2018), and Keister and Southgate (2022). For our purposes, suffice it to say that your starting point in life has an undue influence on the outcomes of your professional efforts. That does not prevent us from admiring and aspiring to the myth of "building something from nothing" as seen in the success stories of people like Elon Musk, Jeff Bezos, and Bill Gates. When recounting those stories, people might forget the ascriptive factors that positioned those leaders to build their empires. The myth of meritocracy, the idea that our societies reward arduous work above all else, is pervasive. Sociology has studied how the culture of modernity and capitalism makes it quite easy for successful individuals to think that the world is a meritocracy. Even the most skeptical among us are tempted to think that our accomplishments are the result of some internal qualities like talent or perseverance. Our failures, in contrast, are always the consequence of external conditions. This bias is commonly known in psychology as self-serving bias, a mechanism to make us feel more positive about ourselves. Privilege is always more recognizable in others than in ourselves.

And while the idea that everybody gets what they deserve is a myth, there are proven ways to help you achieve your goals. Education is one. Engaging in the work of getting a university degree improves your opportunity "space." Of course, neither educational opportunities nor all degrees are equally distributed. For certain occupations, organizations, and bureaucratic levels (think CEO), the prestige of the institution you are attending matters. Employers are incapable of knowing the quality of your education, so they rely on the traditional prestige of the institutions as a proxy for assessing your training skills. As previously mentioned, the prestige of certain majors, regardless of the actual skills transmitted, provides another prestige advantage when applying for jobs.

You have little control over your background or the prestige of your university or your major. Hopefully, efforts like those outlined in this book will help collectively raise the prestige of Sociology among employers. For now, it is up to you to actively construct the image and value of the sociologist in the minds of employers. You might still partially believe in the myth of meritocracy and that a better society is inherently more meritocratic than that of today. That may lead you to think that "good people" should base their achievements on merits. The idea of networking may make you feel that you are contributing to an unjust society.

However, when it comes to social transformation and career development goals, guilt is a useless emotion. Learn to get rid of it. Remember that networks still have an informational value, helping you process vast amounts of information. The Internet may give you access to almost infinite opportunities, but it does not help you find or evaluate them. Networking is more likely to even the playing field or give you an edge among those equally qualified. Giving up or ignoring opportunities is unlikely to help marginalized populations. The problems of inequality are structural, not just the aggregate of individual behavior. It is possible to develop and enact highly effective networks that also contribute to more just societies. Taking advantage of better opportunities allows you to help others. Finally, networking is an instrument for promoting Sociology. If you believe as I do that sociological thinking can help leaders in the private, nonprofit, and government sectors make better decisions, then your job is to promote that view among others. Let go of the guilt and start seeing networking as part of your sociological responsibility.

Anxiety and Lack of Scripts

One of the hallmarks of twenty-first-century social relationships in America is their ever-increasing informality. This is due partly to the rejection of social scripts about events and interactions. The lack of scripts implies more freedom to spontaneously approach others. It also heightens the sense of authenticity of interactions and dismisses scripts as "false." That gain in freedom and authenticity comes at the price of greater uncertainty and ambiguity. Without scripts, people behave in less expected ways. Without the use of scripts in networking, you may encounter pervasive ambiguity and have trouble reading social situations and knowing how to react accordingly (Ball-Rokeach, 1973). You may also have difficulty defining the purpose or goal of the interaction, referred to as focused ambiguity. Is it about making friends or business contacts? If both, how are you supposed to proceed? Not surprisingly, the greater the uncertainty, the greater your anxiety about approaching people. The lack of scripts increases the amount of improvisation needed during interactions, amping up the anxiety level further still. Avoiding contact is the only sure way to eradicate the anxiety. I propose instead that you manage your anxiety by creating your own scripts.

Creating Your Own Scripts

The word script may suggest a mechanical, unthinking conversation with predetermined responses. For example, we casually ask how people are doing and expect them to answer, "Good, thank you," regardless of how they really feel. Think of scripts as a somewhat more flexible tool—recommendations for how to start or continue interactions that still allow for a certain level of spontaneity and authenticity. Some recommendations for scripts follow.

Establish a Connection When talking to people you don't know, looking for and emphasizing commonalities is the best way to jumpstart a relationship. For professional networking, the best commonality is to have a similar career "project" or "cause." In this case that would be your interest in the industry, organization, or position. Sharing majors or alma maters is a traditional way to establish possible commonalities. These traditional sources of "connection" tend toward homogeneous ties. The one exception is heterogeneity of age, providing you with connections to older individuals with already established careers. But you can also find commonalities even when talking to diverse potential contacts. One advantage of modern societies is that in addition to the number of identities associated with race, gender, ethnicity, and class, current culture offers a myriad of identity-creating elements. Sports, for example, continues to offer a key point of possible connection across groups. So are media content, food, and hobbies.

The most difficult ties to create are to those at the highest levels of the social hierarchy. In his famous book, *Distinction: A Social Critique of the Judgement of Taste*, Pierre Bourdieu (1984) explores how elites use taste to create cohesive and exclusionary practices. While these practices still exist, modern elites have diversified tastes, providing more opportunities for connection. You may still need to learn how to play golf if you want to become a CEO or a prestigious corporate lawyer. However, most people allow themselves guilty and common pleasures like watching the Housewives shows or baking. Such activities offer opportunities for connections.

Ask Interesting Questions Most of us are happy to talk about ourselves, our ideas, and our accomplishments. That is why it is important to do research before a networking event to help you find questions that may be of real interest to you and help create a significant connection. Paying attention to what people are saying and asking follow-up questions helps deepen a connection. Furthermore, good questions display your diligence and analytical skills.

Offer Sincere Praise This is an area of social life that I personally find difficult. In Mexican culture, it is common to praise the boss or any authority figure as part of the theater of social life. In the United States, I have noticed an attitude of "how great we all are" in which positive thinking reinforces group dynamics. I can't help but cringe in these situations. My own natural outlook as a sociologist is to focus on the negative, and to only give praise when I think it is merited. But we should all work on praising others. In social situations, complimenting others on their accomplishments and what they offer is a powerful tool and an inherent ingredient of good relationships. No one wants to be in contact with someone who constantly reminds us of our failings, deserved or not. As part of networking strategies, but also because I want to be a positive force for others, I try to praise others more often. My own internal requirement is that the praise be real, not fake. There are some clear issues that you should avoid, even in praise. Physical characteristics or things like hair, clothing, and make-up are usually off the table, unless thematically relevant to the interaction. Do not mention people's age directly or indirectly unless they do it first. Praise the quality of their experiences instead.

Be Formal in Early Conversations Despite the informal nature of modern social interactions, professional situations tend to require a more traditional formality. While many networking opportunities may appear to be informal (such as a reception), you are still expected to follow professional standards of conduct. Remember, many of these standards may be assumed and not explicit. Some general recommendations to follow when approaching potential contacts include:

- Asking if the person has time or an inclination for the interaction;
- Introducing yourself and saying why you want to talk to them;
- Using the person's last name and title until they indicate otherwise;
- Avoiding politics or religion unless the event or contact makes it a natural point of conversation;
- Being inclusive and aware of other people;
- Thanking the person for their time.

Keep an Eye on Social Cues This is the most difficult and anxiety-creating aspect of conversing with strangers and acquaintances. Some people may not want to talk to anybody. Their lack of reciprocity in the conversation signals their disinterest. But coming out of the pandemic, some of us are a little rusty in reviving our social skills. Try to jumpstart the conversation two or three times and if there is no response, excuse yourself to talk to someone else. Also be aware of when to leave. You may be having a remarkably interesting conversation, but if other people are waiting to access that person you may need to cut it short. This is especially important if someone of higher status than you is waiting to break in or if your conversation partner seems to want to talk to them; it is expected (although never explicitly stated) that you cede your turn to them. Not wanting to monopolize your contact's time may offer a great segue to ask them for an appointment or permission to contact them in the future.

Request Future Contact This piece of advice is useful at the end of conversations when you want to continue the relationship. It provides a "next step" as part of the networking process. For example, you may want to continue the contact to expand your conversation about a topic. Once upon a time you would have exchanged business cards. Now, you just need to make sure that their email address is publicly available and that you have permission to contact them that way later. Emailing is also useful when seeking information concerning another contact associated with them, such as the name of the person in charge of internships or a potential contact in another department or role.

Do Not Ask Directly for a Job Directly asking for a job in a networking situation can be uncomfortable. The rules governing informational interviews, a tool of both career development and networking, explicitly forbid asking directly for a job. However, if the other party mentions a vacancy or a search, then you are allowed to ask for more details to see if it matches your situation. Some possible questions might be:

- Is there a particular person in your organization/department that I should talk to about an internship?
- Do you have any contacts in Department X (not the contact's department) that I could approach about x, y, or z?
- Do you know of other organizations like yours that I should explore?

The Power of Email

During an internship as part of my Communication major circa 1995, I was lucky to assist in the creation of a special magazine celebrating the 400th anniversary of Monterrey, Mexico's founding. As part of the project, I was asked to contact the CEOs of major local corporations to ask for profiles, photographs, and other information. I still remember the anxiety I felt phoning what seemed to me to be "the most important people." I had an almost pathological fear of cold-calling random people, let alone important ones. I ended up speaking to their secretaries, who were nice to me. Subsequent changes in technology have transformed both the use of phones and the roles of secretaries (now called the more neutral administrative assistants). A higher proportion of executives and workers are now expected to manage their schedules and emails personally. In addition, email contact information can be obtained publicly.

Random emailing a stranger may not produce the result you want; some people may not respond at all. You are more likely to get a reply if your request matches the contact's experience. But even then, people are busy and get many emails. Following the principles of the two step-flow of communication theory can help increase your odds of getting a response. Originally developed to explain voter behavior, the theory posits that a mass media message becomes more effective when you add a second step: reinforcement of the message by someone directly connected to the individual (Katz, 1957). Similarly, your email message becomes more effective if you have had a prior in-person interaction with the individual or if you mention a connection to someone in their network.

A note of caution about social media: it can become all-consuming. Even when you use it to stay informed, keep it to a limit; continue to maintain your contacts with friends and colleagues and to reach new contacts. Social media is no substitute for in-person social interaction, and it can be an obstacle for both your job productivity and the quality of your personal life. Create and respect personal boundaries. Only post professionally related information on LinkedIn.

Conclusion

Networking differs from community building in its instrumental orientation. Social capital, the instrumental side of social relationships, has various positive effects for individuals and communities. Sociology majors tend to avoid networking because it creates anxiety and guilt. Creating social scripts to guide your interactions can help diminish the anxiety of interacting with strangers. A combination of electronic and personal contacts works best when approaching an individual for networking purposes.

Discussion Questions

1. Is it possible to modify how individuals create networks in a culture? Do you think it is ethical? How comfortable do you feel approaching strangers?
2. What is/are your personal privilege(s)? Do you ever feel guilty about them?
3. What is your opinion on the use of social scripts?
4. What is your opinion about the effect of social scripts for society?
5. What components of the social scripts mentioned in this chapter will you adopt? Which ones will you discard?
6. How do you currently address people with more authority than you?

Action/Reflection Activity

1. Part I. Review the information available about your university's Career Center advisor and make an appointment with somebody responsible for the major or sector/industry you're interested in. Discuss the types of jobs and organizations available. Ask for the best way to locate and contact alumni from your major.

Table 5.1 Sample questions for informational interview

Can you tell me about a typical day on the job?	What are employers typically looking for when hiring people in this line of work?
How did you get started doing this type of work?	What kind of internship would prepare me for work in this area?
What is your favorite part of your job? What is your least favorite part of your job?	My background and experience is X (briefly note your major qualifications). How does that compare with employers' expectations when hiring in this industry?
What surprised you the most when you started working in this field?	May I have your business card?
What is the typical starting salary for someone in this line of work?	Can I request to become one of your LinkedIn contacts?
How do you see this industry developing in the future? How is your industry changing?	Is there anything else you think is important that I should be aware of?
What advice would you give to someone who wants to get started in this industry?	Is there anyone else I might talk to about this?

2. Part II. Using the alumni contacts method, select and contact an alum of interest:
   (a) Develop a script for the interview containing the elements described in this chapter.
   (b) Research the organization and alumni personal histories.
   (c) Plan an informational interview that does not repeat public information and helps resolve your doubts about potential jobs.
   (d) Perform the informational interview. While an in-person visit to the workplace of the person would be ideal, telephone or Zoom are also good. See Table 5.1 for sample questions.
   (e) Write a post-interview reflection. What have you learned about your potential career path? What next steps should you take?

Works Cited

Ball-Rokeach, S. J. (1973). From pervasive ambiguity to a definition of the situation. *Sociometry, 36*(3), 378–389.

Bourdieu, P. (1984). *Distinction: A social critique of the judgement of taste.* Harvard University Press.

Burt, R. S. (2000). The network structure of social capital. *Research in Organizational Behavior, 22,* 345–423.

Burt, R. S. (2009). The contingent value of social capital. In *Knowledge and social capital: Foundations and applications* (pp. 255–286). Routledge.

Burt, R. S. (2018). Structural holes. In *Social Stratification* (pp. 659–663). Routledge.

Burt, R. S., Hogarth, R. M., & Michaud, C. (2000). The social capital of French and American managers. *Organizations Science, 11*(2), 123–147.

Coleman, J. S. (1988). Social capital in the creation of human capital. *American Journal of Sociology, 94*, S95–S120.

Cross, J. L. M., & Lin, N. (2008). *Access to social capital and status attainment in the United States: Racial/ethnic and gender differences* (pp. 364–379). An international research program.

Dahlgren, P. (2000). The Internet and the democratization of civic culture. *Political Communication, 17*(4), 335–340.

DiMaggio, P., Hargittai, E., Neuman, W. R., & Robinson, J. P. (2001). Social implications of the Internet. *Annual Review of Sociology, 27*(1), 307–336.

Gittell, J. H., & Weiss, L. (2004). Coordination networks within and across organizations: A multi-level framework. *Journal of Management Studies, 41*(1), 127–153.

Granovetter, M. S. (1973). The strength of weak ties. *American Journal of Sociology, 78*(6), 1360–1380.

Heckscher, C. (1994). Defining the post-bureaucratic type. In *Sociology of organizations. Structures and relationships* (pp. 98–106). Sage.

Katz, E. (1957). The two-step flow of communication: An up-to-date report on an hypothesis. *Public Opinion Quarterly, 21*(1), 61–78.

Keister, L. A., & Southgate, D. E. (2022). *Inequality: A contemporary approach to race, class, and gender*. Cambridge University Press.

Manley, J. E. (2000). Negotiating quality: Total quality management and the complexities of transforming professional organizations. *Sociological Forum, 15*(3), 457–484.

Pfeffer, F. T., & Killewald, A. (2018). Generations of advantage. Multigenerational correlations in family wealth. *Social Forces, 96*(4), 1411–1442.

Pichler, F., & Wallace, C. (2009). Social capital and social class in Europe: The role of social networks in social stratification. *European Sociological Review, 25*(3), 319–332.

Putnam, R. D. (2000). *Bowling alone: The collapse and revival of American community*. Simon and Schuster.

Rajkumar, K., Saint-Jacques, G., Bojinov, I., Brynjolfsson, E., & Aral, S. (2022). A causal test of the strength of weak ties. *Science, 377*(6612), 1304–1310.

Savage, M. (2021). *The return of inequality*. Harvard University Press.

Sensenbrenner, J., & Portes, A. (2018). Embeddedness and immigration: Notes on the social determinants of economic action. In *The sociology of economic life* (pp. 93–115). Routledge.

Woolcock, M., & Narayan, D. (2000). Social capital: Implications for development theory, research, and policy. *The World Bank Research Observer, 15*(2), 225–249.

Part II
Transferable Skills

A Sociological View of the Resume 6

This second part of the book looks at transferable skills in the context of the job application process. The recontextualization work explored in this section includes identifying your transferable skills and supporting experiences to include in a job application. Those skills, along with evidence that you have them, can be turned into instruments and formats generally accepted by employers and managers.

The first step in the application process is submitting a professional resume. After that, you usually progress through a series of interviews, starting with Human Resources professionals and ending in a meeting with potential bosses and colleagues. In addition to interviews, some companies ask applicants to make a presentation on a topic related to the organization. Some also administer personality, cognitive, and skills tests, depending on the position. Those tests may take place any time in the process after you have submitted a resume. The deceptively simple resume is a key part of the process, so we will explore its intricacies through several chapters. This chapter will describe its main purpose and components. Chapter 7 will concentrate on how to express sociological skills and how to showcase other transferable skills using the language of business. Chapter 8 will discuss adapting the Skills section of the resume to fit the position you desire.

This chapter presents a sociological view of the explicit and implicit functions of the resume, examining it both as a rational tool for the purposes of different actors and as part of a capitalist system of production. It identifies its functions and how Human Resources professionals use it to process the information. It will offer a basic framework for what to consider when developing your resume and how you can use the resume's different elements to reflect your best self for a particular job. Remember, there is no such a thing as a "perfect resume." It is an individual tool that balances different instrumental goals, follows sometimes ambiguous standards, and expresses individual identity. That said, I have included three sample resumes developed by Sociology students during their late sophomore year as guides—real students showcasing their best selves to the labor market and presenting their interests.

Before starting, I want to acknowledge the natural feelings of anxiety and vulnerability that often accompany the job application process, particularly for students trying to enter the workforce for the first time. Sending applications into the black box of the labor market and getting no response can make you feel uncertain and rejected. But whether a first-time or a more experienced job-hunter, your challenge is not to get a job, but to find one that can launch you on your desired career path. I have known people who obtained a job with their first and only application; others have taken a year and submitted more than a hundred different applications to land a job. The "failure" of one or multiple applications does not correlate with the strength of your skills or your potential future success. Even with high qualifications and following every recommendation in this book, you cannot be assured of getting the job you want. However, there are clear steps you can take to increase your chances.

One thing to keep in mind is the needs of those on the other side of the job-hunting divide: the Human Resources practitioners in charge of recruitment and selection. They also feel anxious about their part of the process. Their job is to find people who can do the job, "fit" the organization, and not pose problems. Seldom does a hiring professional get credit for finding a superstar, but they can be fired for hiring the wrong person. All the managerial techniques developed to guide the hiring process are aimed at controlling the uncontrollable. They generate incomplete information about the quality and fit of a potential employee. The only sure way to know if a candidate is qualified is to hire them and have them do the work. Because of incomplete information and uncontrollable outcomes, Human Resources professionals have a negative bias. They will be hypersensitive to potential signals indicating that a candidate is not a good bet. Just as in any other social process, some signals may be directly connected to your quality as a future worker while others may be only partly related to potential performance. These signals may be cultural practices unrelated to performance at all. Regardless of their connection to your future performance, all signals are important during the application process.

Explicit and Implicit Functions of the Resume

Explicit functions in modern organizations assume the presence of rational actors who are taking purposeful actions to achieve a goal. But as any sociologist knows, we humans are not perfectly rational. Students sometimes see the resume as a tool for expressing one's authentic self. They want their resumes to display their unique point of view. Individual expression is indeed one component; an effective resume needs to also reflect the needs and biases of employers. Despite all the research done about their behaviors, Human Resources people tend to believe that they are completely rational when analyzing a resume. They think they are using the best tools to find the best candidates. In their minds, their tools are always, and only, merit-based. They tend to ignore the limits of human information processing and the ways in which the economic system and culture affect our behaviors. Even when Human Resources personnel are aware of implicit functions and biases, it is difficult for them to make practical corrections to their own behavior because of social pressures regarding "best" practices and fear of failure. This is not evidence of maliciousness or a lack of fairness; Human Resources personnel share the same biases and responses to social pressures common to all people living in society, sociologists included.

The explicit function of the resume for an applicant is to get a job interview. It is one of the most universal hurdles for entrance into the labor market (at least in Western countries). For organizations, it is to gather enough information to infer an applicant's skills, expertise, and potential, and to assess their likelihood of fitting into the organization or position in the least amount of time. From a sociological perspective, the resume is a tool of modernity and capitalism; more precisely, it is one of management and Human Resources practices.

While the explicit functions of the resume are supposed to concentrate on skills, expertise, and qualifications, Sociology and Psychology have both found that it fulfills other latent functions. Hiring managers often do not recognize these other purposes, which can lead to unintended consequences. Understanding and utilizing the latent functions of the resume described below can increase your chances of finding a job by anticipating potential biases and problems.

Reflect a General Capacity for Efficiency One of the most fundamental elements of capitalism is the significance it places on efficiency as a moral value (Giddens, 1990). Efficiency is usually interpreted in terms of "cost," using the least amount of resources to accomplish a task. For the resume, this means minimizing reading time and space used. Some resume elements and practices are symbols of future efficiency; they represent a person's capacity to perform other work-related tasks. Efficiency in the form of readability allows hiring managers to exert minimal effort when reviewing as many as a couple hundred resumes by sifting through relevant information as fast as possible. Readability, good writing, and efficiency are closely linked; we can process information better when it is presented in a familiar format with good grammar.

Allow Recruiters to Infer Your Personality Managerial Psychology has found that managers and Human Resources personnel take information in the resume and attribute personality traits to the author. These traits are usually framed in psychological dimensions such as extroversion, conscientiousness, openness to experience, agreeableness, and neuroticism. Most studies in Business Psychology agree that conscientiousness (the tendency to be responsible, organized, hard-working, goal-directed, and adhere to norms and rules) affects the perceived employability of a candidate. Some evidence also indicates that perceptions of extroversion and openness to change also increase chances of getting an interview (Burns et al., 2014). The problem is that employers may be misreading your personality. The only dimension in which the candidate's self-evaluation and the employer's attribution have been shown to match (that is, what employers think of the candidate through a resume is the same as what the candidates think about themselves) is in the area of extroversion (Cole et al., 2009). From the vantage point of the sociologist, homophily is another element where perceived personality traits may affect the chance of securing an interview. Although this term meaning "love of sameness" (Lazarsfeld & Merton, 1954) originally was applied to friendship, the concept also explains our preference to interact with those who are like ourselves. What people call "organizational fit" is really homophily. Notwithstanding proclamations in support of diversity, homophily remains a potent force in hiring decisions.

Reflect One's Capacity for Conformity As with any other artifact related to modernity, many current elements in the resume are based on tradition. The original "efficiency" rationale behind a practice may no longer apply and be lost in time. Efficiency and tradition are difficult to differentiate in organizational practice. The main personality trait associated with employability is your capacity to follow rules carefully. In other words, conscientiousness is conformity. That includes how you structure your resume. When I help students with their resumes, I often face resistance when suggesting small changes. They question the need for random changes that have no bearing on the content or readability of the resume. What does it really matter if you abbreviate the months in listing your job history? Or if you use past tense rather than present to describe your current job? In truth, it *shouldn't* matter. But to people who review and select resumes, it can produce a negative bias; any small deviation from the standard format is potentially disqualifying. They must eliminate applicants in some way. Sticking with the conventional format is a safe strategy.

Provide Cues Regarding Class, Gender, Sexual Orientation, Race, and Ethnicity A strong body of sociological literature offers empirical evidence showing that discrimination by race, gender, ethnicity, and sexual orientation occurs during the resume evaluation process (Pager et al., 2009; Mishel, 2016; Quillian & Midtbøen, 2021). Something as simple as a person's name can provide clues about someone's membership in social categories and affect their chances of being invited for an interview. While direct discrimination can still be an issue in hiring, unconscious bias related to race-neutral cultural preferences is a widespread problem. Certain skills and personalities are often associated with particular social groups. In Western countries, and all over the world, markers of efficiency, merit, and cognitive ability overlap with characteristics attributed to high status white males. We know, for example, that individuals of Asian heritage are often seen as "lacking personality" because they tend to score lower in the extroversion measure of personality tests. African Americans may be perceived as more "radical," which could imply less conscientiousness (although it might really mean less tolerance for racially motivated mistreatment). Women are usually considered to have less ability for highly complex cognitive tasks. Limited research indicates that the resumes of heterosexual males are evaluated as more employable, and lesbian women and gay men are seen as more employable than heterosexual women (Horvath & Ryan, 2003). Of course, these trends are societal averages; there is much variation by sector and industry, and across and within organizations.

Elements of the Resume

The resume is an institutionalized instrument that contains components of specific interest to the organization in question. As with any cultural product, expectations change over time. At this moment, the most expected elements of a resume required of those transitioning from school to work are listed below.

Basic Information Name, email, telephone number, and LinkedIn profile.

Academic History Majors, minors, GPA, academic awards, relevant classes, relevant projects, and student group participation.

Conference Presentations, Papers, and Certificates Include any formal courses or certifications from an educational institution apart from traditional academic degrees. You may also highlight certifications and courses outside your degree in the Skills section of the resume.

Work Experience Each item you list should include basic information: position title, organization, start and end dates, a bullet list of the activities you performed in the position along with an achievement if possible. Location (city, state) is optional, but it is best to include the country if it was outside the US.

Volunteer Experience and Other Extracurriculars Extracurriculars refers to any hobby or side activity that you have pursued intensively. If it was done under the sponsorship of the educational institution where you got a degree, include it either here or in the Academic History area. This is the most flexible section of the resume. Revise the title or the content to best reflect your experience or to fit the job you seek.

Skills Socioemotional, Transferable, Technical.

Optional Elements Personal or Summary Statement, Photo, Design Layout.

Figure 6.1 presents a resume developed by Nicole Bennett, a Sociology major in her junior year. She is interested in the social aspects of Urban Planning and Development, particularly how people use spaces for public social interaction. This is a template resume; Nicole will modify it later to better fit the position she applies for.

Normally, recruiters pay most attention to Work Experience where they look for the skills and expertise associated with the posted position. If relevant work experience is missing, recruiters will next turn to Academic History and Volunteering/Extracurriculars in search of applicable skills and expertise. You should therefore pay close attention to these sections if your work experience is limited. They are also critical if you are trying to change your career trajectory or industry.

What does Nicole's resume show? Her use of an expected BA date instantly announces that she is still a student with some time to go before finishing her degree. If she is applying for internships, part-time jobs and/or entry-level jobs, that

Nicole Bennett

1350 Court Drive, Sunnydale, IL 50555 | (723) 723-4102 | bennettnic@gmail.com
LinkedIn Profile: linkedin.com/in/nicole-bennett-5a3b221a2

Education:
DePaul University, Chicago, IL — *BA in Sociology* – Exp. Spring 2022
 Relevant Coursework: Urban Sociology, Race, Ethnicity, and Housing Seminar, and Cities and the Environment

Benedict High School, Sunnydale, IL — *High School Diploma* – May 2018
 Extracurriculars: Theater Tech – Built performance sets and did lighting for shows

Experience:
Silver Lake Restaurant, Sunnydale, IL — *Hostess/Carryout* – August 2017 – PRESENT
- Handled multiple customers and responsibilities in fast-paced environment while ensuring exceptional service
- Answered phone calls, put in carry-out orders, registered payments, and made teas and smoothies
- Trained over 8 new employees in the skills listed above and taught them how to work efficiently under pressure

Vincentians in Action Service Immersion, Los Angeles, CA — *Participant* – December 3-10, 2019
- Worked with multiple organizations within Skid Row that dealt with homelessness and explored the contributing factors to this issue such as mental illness, drug abuse, and rising rents
- Served over 800 meals over the course of three days at a Midnight Missions
- Worked as a runner for Meals on Wheels and brought meals to over 30 people across West Hollywood

Santa's Village Azoosment Park, East Dundee, IL — *Zookeeper* – June 2016 – October 2016
- Cleaned and fed over 100 different animals.
- Handled money for souvenirs and animal feed
- Supervised human and animal interactions to maintain safe environment for children and animals

Extracurriculars:
Achieving Immigrant Rights and Equality, *Member,* **2018 – Present**
 Taught conversational ESL class with Spanish-speaking adults in Little Village, Chicago

Urban Farming Organization, *Member,* **2018 – Present**
 Determined most cost/space efficient ways to grow vegetation in an urban area

Youth Leadership Academy, *Member,* **2012 – 2018**
 Conducted annual service projects aimed at bettering the community

Skills:
- Basic Photo Editing and Graphic Design
- Adobe Photoshop and Illustrator
- Cash Handling and Registers

- Customer Service
- Intercultural Communication
- Training and Education

Fig. 6.1 Sample Resume Nicole Bennett

is not likely to be an issue. She mentions classes related to Urban Planning, so she can claim some expertise on the topic. Given her interests, she might seek work for a local government urban planning department. A Sociology degree is not likely to get her hired to design a park or a community center, but qualifies her for an entry-level job such as an administrative assistant or an assistant researcher position in a local urban planning department. Her education has prepared her to write reports and help create models, both physical and virtual. While not her dream job, it would allow her to assess whether that area is really what she wants and to develop her network before or while she continues her education. Her work experience indicates that she collaborates well with people (personal and intercultural communication) and is interested in improving communities. She also has experience training other workers. Even her stint working at a zoo provides the image of someone who can work hard, without adding the words "hard-working" to her resume. While she could add that to the Skills section, she has other, more specific skills that she prefers to emphasize there. Her extracurriculars also highlight her interest in community development. She included her high school experience as a set designer to illustrate that she has skills that can be applied to model-building. Her Skills section reinforces the other elements of the resume.

Recommendations Physical addresses are no longer needed in a resume, and they should be avoided to maintain privacy. Nicole may add a summary statement at the top (just below her name and address), which lists the main skills and qualifications relevant to a job. Including a summary allows you to increase the number of potential words that match the job posting and which may help move your resume into the favorable group. I will talk more about job posting matches in Chap. 9. Nicole may also need to remove her high school information. While college freshmen are encouraged to include their high school information, Nicole is a junior. However, because her high school theater tech experience is relevant, she may include that in the extracurricular section.

Strategies for Developing a Resume

Nicole's resume is simple and solid and can be used as a first-draft template. It should not be considered "perfect" or the model for every Sociology student or every type of position. You will need to call on your critical thinking skills and creativity to shape your own resume. Simple designs are the norm for government and nonprofit organizations unless the position is directly related to graphic design.

Strategies for Developing a Resume 89

Applications to the federal government have their own format, which include more details for all positions. For most organizations, the following strategies may help you design your own resume.

Show and Tell Normally, good writing follows the rule "Show, don't tell." The resume is slightly different. Human Resources professionals do not read deeply; they skim for a few seconds before making a gut decision and moving to the next resume. In some organizations, the first screening of a resume may be done by an unsophisticated computer program searching only for keywords. The system only funnels resumes containing the most keyword hits to the next part of the process. To increase your chances of being noticed, you need to reinforce the message of your skills and expertise without being redundant. Redundancy can be perceived as bad writing or inefficiency. One way to "Show and Tell" is to combine and reinforce skills and expertise in different areas of the resume. You also want to use different words for the same skill to maximize the number of keyword hits. The Skills section offers a unique opportunity to reframe and rephrase your skills and expertise. This will be discussed in greater depth in the Skills section in Chap. 7.

Follow Conventions You might be tempted to modify your resume to make it appear unique and "different" to stand out from competitors. And while companies say they want creativity, they want creativity in certain areas and conformity in others. Remember that there will be other opportunities to show your creative side later in the job application process. The focus should be on the skills set and experience you bring to the position, the team, and the organization. That said, resume conventions are tricky. Sometimes they relate to the explicit and implicit functions of the resume, other times, they are almost inexplicable. We could fill a whole book with resume conventions alone and still not make sense of them. They have come to be taken for granted. I list the most common ones in Table 6.1. However, the best way to discover if you are breaking an expected convention is to ask a career development professional or a worker in the industry to review your resume and tell you if they see anything unusual.

One Size Does *Not* Fit All Using the same resume for all positions and organizations you apply to is not a strong strategy for landing a great job. Create an extended resume that contains all your information. Copy and paste the appropriate elements from that document into a new resume to fit each position you seek. Investigate the target organization's websites and social media accounts to collect knowledge about the organization and its style. Also review your personal networks, including LinkedIn, to identify contacts who might be able to help you.

Table 6.1 List of resume conventions

Resume Conventions and Explanation
Use only one page and one side (Efficiency, Readability)
Display Basic Information on top and make it prominent (Readability)
Follow the Basic Information section with either Work Experience or Education (Efficiency, Readability)
Include expected date of degree completion under Education (Efficiency)
Arrange items within sections in chronological order, starting with the most recent (Readability)
Use the same form of grammar to describe each element within a section (Good Writing)
Use simple bullet points for job and activity descriptions (Readability)
Keep sentences simple and short, but they can extend all the way to the right margin (Efficiency, Readability)
Review and correct all typos, grammar, or spelling mistakes (Good Writing, Efficiency)
Avoid redundancy between job title and description in Work Experience (Good Writing)
Abbreviate months (Efficiency)
Avoid adjectives, particularly when referring to yourself, such as excellent worker (Good Writing)
Start each sentence with a verb (Efficiency)
Include job dates (Readability)
Use both lowercase and uppercase letters except on section titles (Readability)

Modify your resume to reflect the information you glean in your investigations and tailor your resumes based on industry or type of position.

Overestimate, But Don't Lie We sociologists devote much attention to detecting direct and indirect discrimination in job applications and work environments. As a job applicant and eventually a supervisor of others, you need to consider your own internalization of social biases. Our cousins in Psychology label this Impostor Syndrome to describe a feeling of not belonging, a lack of confidence in one's skills and achievements, and the sinking sense of being a fraud (Martins & Anthony, 2007). Impostor Syndrome is more likely to afflict women (Calvard, 2018), minorities (Dancy & Jean-Marie, 2014), and individuals from working-class backgrounds (Warnock, 2016). Equally real is discrimination against Sociology in comparison with other disciplines. You may hear people imply that it is not a real science (usually coming from the Natural Sciences folks), not practical enough (from Managerial Science majors), not radical enough (from the Humanities), and not clear enough (from general audiences). That may leave you feeling insecure about your skills and the relevancy of your experience. I recommend slightly overestimating your skills when you write a resume. Remember, the resume is just an introductory document. You and the organization will have opportunities later to

Strategies for Developing a Resume

assess the fit between you. To reduce feelings of anxiety, you might also talk to a faculty member or a career development professional about how to characterize your level of experience, skills, and expertise.

Omitting Is Not Lying You do not owe your employers your whole being, just the one that shows up to work. The job-seeking process comes with a social understanding that, just as the employer has negative biases, candidates try to show their best, not their complete, selves. After a candidate is hired and develops a relationship with the employer, more disclosure may follow. Because of the short time they dedicate to each resume, many reviewers do not even notice career gaps. Career gaps during the pandemic years are expected.

Be Aware of Potential Biases As a sociologist, you are an expert in discrimination and biases. Being aware of them will help you decide your best course of action. You can decide to modify your resume to avoid biases as much as possible. Or you can choose the opposite route and use your resume as a sort of test to see if the organization is the right environment for you. There is no right or wrong approach. Some Sociology majors decide they only want to work with organizations with anti-racist, anti-discrimination policies and practices. While all companies say they do not discriminate, only a few follow their own stated values. The resume may be a test to see which companies follow through with their good intentions. Some students, particularly at the beginning of their careers, just want to get a foot in the door, thinking they will have better opportunities to choose their preferred work environments later. Those candidates do their best to present a "self" that matches organizational expectations. No research is available about which strategy is more effective; choose according to your preference and goals.

Figure 6.2 shows a resume for another Sociology major, my former student, Gina Foster. Gina is a double major in Sociology and Psychology. She wants a job promoting the socioemotional development of children. When she created this resume, she was not sure what kind of positions were available in that area. Given her uncertainty, she decided to emphasize her other major, Psychology, and those pertinent classes. Gina's Experience section showcases her passion and expertise in the area of child development. From the resume, we can see that her profile combines scientist/activist orientations. She shows obvious interest in learning new things about child development, both for her personal knowledge and to create more effective interventions. She also has graphic and writing skills useful in disseminating findings to general audiences. This resume is very good for someone who would like to do project evaluation work in a nonprofit organization. She also

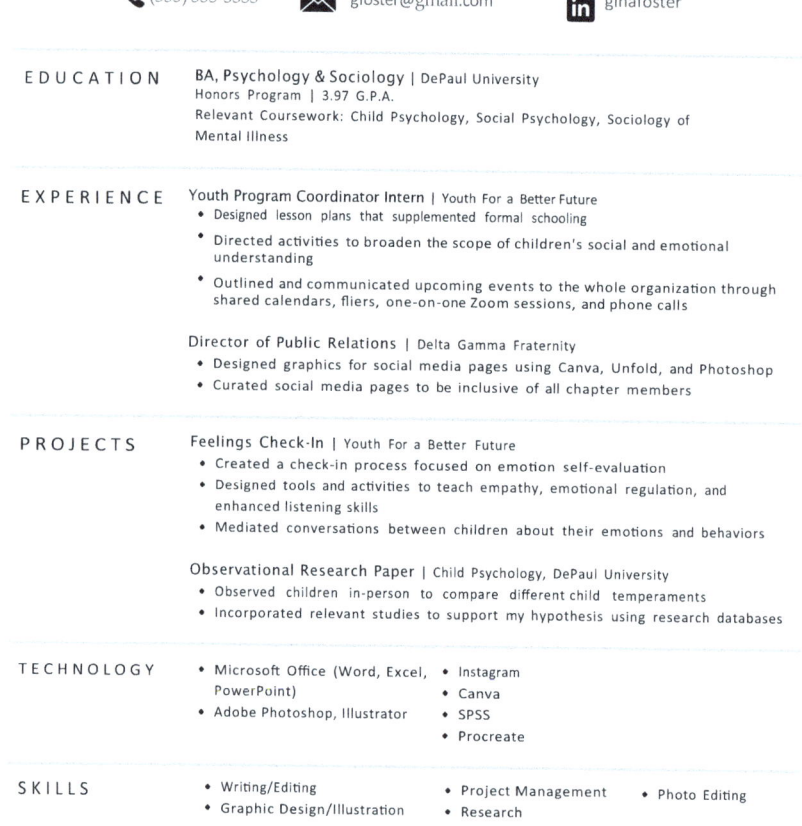

Fig. 6.2 Sample Resume Gina Foster

shows managerial skills. In this version of her resume, she put less emphasis on her sociological skills. Once she has a more specific position in mind, she may decide to flip the emphasis to foreground Sociology rather than Psychology. While she follows many resume conventions, she also takes some liberties in her section names. For example, instead of Extracurricular or Volunteer Activities, she emphasized her research work. She also separated her technical from her other skills to give that more attention.

Recommendations My biggest recommendation for Gina is to include dates for potential graduation, Experience, and Projects. Length of time in a particular activity is an important aspect of experience, and omitting dates may give the impression that she is either hiding something or is imprecise. She also needs to include the locations of organizations. Another suggestion is to be more specific about her research skills. Instead of simply stating "Research" in the Skills section, she could emphasize her observational research or child development research. Her sociological skills could include quantitative data analysis and other qualitative techniques. Another way to enhance her research skills section would be to include the terms Program Evaluation or Intervention Evaluation to emphasize the applied nature of her research focus.

A final sample resume, shown in Fig. 6.3, comes from one of my sophomore students, Daniela Saavedra. At the time, she was exploring careers in Sociology and was open to many possibilities. She opted for a two-column resume template, which offers a little more control over how information is presented. It also helps maximize space. Some Career Centers discourage the use of a two-column resume, thinking it may create ambiguity in how readers process the information. Having two starting lines makes it harder to skim. In my experience, students are attracted to templates because of their ease of use. You may consider creating your own template to give you more flexibility in organizing the information. You may notice that Daniela has space at the bottom of the first column to add more information. She is using the Education section to communicate her interest in improving educational experiences. She is also emphasizing her quantitative and qualitative research classes. While her Work Experience is not necessarily relevant to her career plans after graduation, it does express her interest in education and communication skills. Her time as Sociology Club president adds valuable organizational, managerial, and leadership skills information.

Recommendations To strengthen Daniela's research skills claims, I would recommend adding a Projects subsection to the Education section highlighting the

DANIELA SAAVEDRA

DETAILS

PHONE
3127144934

EMAIL
danisaaverda@gmail.com

SKILLS

Project Management

Analytical Thinking

Creative Problem Solving

Intercultural Communication

Adaptability

Leadership

TECHNOLOGY

Microsoft Word, PowerPoint, and Excel

Google Docs, Slides, Sheets, and Forms

SPSS

EDUCATION

BA, Sociology, DePaul University — Chicago
Sep 2018 — Exp. Jun 2022

Minor in Political Science | 3.86 G.P.A.

Relevant Coursework: Transformative Justice, Sociology of Education, Multiculturalism in Education, Quantitative and Qualitative Research

EMPLOYMENT HISTORY

Babysitter
Jan 2016 — Present

- Supervised children during parents' working hours, including some nights and weekends
- Designed educational activities such as Word of the Day in which the child identifies the letters and practices writing the word in English and Spanish
- Ensured child's safety and health by keeping the home clean and monitoring activities

Brand Representative, Abercrombie Kids — Chicago
Aug 2019 — Jan 2020

- Anticipated customer needs about store merchandise, promotions, and sales
- Established and maintained a welcoming environment for customers by warmly greeting clients
- Responded to customer problems with trouble-shooting abilities

VOLUNTEERING & EXTRA-CURRICULARS

President, Sociology Club — Chicago
Sep 2019 — Present

- Organized and facilitated weekly advisory board meetings and club events
- Managed club website by validating new members, sharing upcoming events and answering direct messages
- Served as an ambassador between club's advisory board and university's Student Involvement Department

Mentor, Cities Mentor Project — Chicago
Sep 2019 — Jun 2020

- Mentored nine-year old student to develop healthy coping skills
- Offered guidance and a safe space to share personal and academic challenges
- Provided tutoring in Language Arts and Math
- Collaborated with other mentors to ensure the emotional and physical safety of students during mentoring sessions

Fig. 6.3 Sample Resume Daniela Saavedra

topics and methods she employed in her class assignments. As she progresses further in her education, she needs to add more specific experiences that orient her toward the beginning of a career. As an alternative, this section could have been called Research Experience. She also violates the rule about omitting adjectives when she mentions her "excellent trouble shooting abilities." She may want to consider rephrasing that skill.

You may have noticed that none of the resumes includes a personal statement. A couple years ago, including a personal statement (also called an objective or summary statement in non-academic contexts) was considered a key strategy for getting an interview, but current trends give it less attention. A summary statement has one clear advantage, which is to increase the number of words associated with the job posting. This is particularly helpful when computers are used to do the initial filtering of the application and are basically just counting words.

The three resumes included in this chapter are examples of different resume design philosophies. Nicole's illustrates a simple resume, something that could be done with very basic word-processing skills. Gina decided to add color and a couple of images but kept her design very simple too. Daniela used a more flexible and complicated design but kept it in black and white. Although research on the topic is limited (Arnulf et al., 2010), more complicated designs do not increase your chances of being selected and may affect readability. There is one exception, however: the design itself showcases skills. Nicole is "telling" employers she can use graphic design software, but she could show them the same thing by presenting a more sophisticated design. On the other hand, for students trying to portray a rigorous, "scientific" identity conducive to data analysis jobs, to use a complicated design may project an image of "fluffiness" and a lack of seriousness. A simple design is the safest choice. Career Centers also recommend using a simple design for resumes directed toward government and nonprofit organizations.

Conclusion

The resume is a deceptively simple tool. The information itself is not difficult to generate and its format has become a standardized physical expression of modern capitalism and management practices. While it may appear to provide a platform for self-expression, it primarily prioritizes evidence of efficiency and conformity, admitting a dash of merit through the showcasing of skills and expertise. However, think of the resume also as your first opportunity to develop and practice a new, professional "habitus" that recognizes the constraints faced by jobseekers within the capitalist world while also offering opportunities to exercise agency. The first step in achieving the career you want and the eventual power to help others is to carefully think through, design, and calibrate your resume. Take this step seriously and use it as an opportunity to develop a professional identity that suits your aspirations.

Discussion Questions

1. How does the idea of applying for a job make you feel? How can you explain that reaction through sociological thinking?
2. In your opinion, is conformity really a sign of future job performance?
3. Is personality a real component of job performance or more social convention? If you already have an idea of what job you want, is the expectation of certain personality traits a valid requirement for that position?
4. Are there any specific biases in the application process that worry you personally?
5. What is your preferred strategy for dealing with biases: to write your resume either in a way to avoid them or to use them as a test to discover whether the organization is a good fit for you?
6. What social convention listed in Table 6.1 makes the least sense to you?
7. Why do you think jobseekers may avoid customizing their resumes to fit each position?
8. What resume design would you use and why?
9. Think about how you would explain Sociology to a potential employer. Did you include complex and specific verbs?

Action/Reflection Activity

The first step to begin designing your resume is to collect an exhaustive list of your experiences in and outside of school. Spending a couple hours thinking through and answering the following questions about your history should uncover the building materials to create a strong resume. Be bold and try not to worry about how competent you feel in any given area. Employers will know that as a current student or recent graduate your experience in any specific job is limited. Instead, they need to see your potential and who you are as a person. The questions below are based on a model originally generated by experts in experiential learning (Stoddard & Pfeifer, 2018).

1. Identify at least three characteristics in your personal background that provide you with more knowledge or skills than other people may have (i.e., being born in Mexico gives you knowledge of Mexican culture, being a first-generational college student/graduate gives you knowledge of the challenges faced by similar colleagues, such as having a brother with autism provides first-hand experience on how to meet his needs). Any personal characteristic of social categorization (class, gender, race, education, mental health conditions, physical conditions, etc.) can be an expertise.
2. Identify at least three of your passions or hobbies. These can be anything, from reading science fiction to gardening.
3. Name all the clubs or organizations (including sports organizations) you belong to or have belonged to in the past.
4. Identify the artistic activities you have practiced.
5. Make a list of all the jobs you ever had, no matter how informal. Include the title, organization, dates of employment, and activities you performed.
6. List your three favorite classes or topics within Sociology and why.
7. List any major or minors other than Sociology that you are pursuing and why.
8. List your five favorite classes outside Sociology.
9. List all your technical skills, particularly those related to technology and managerial tasks.
10. Identify at least three topics or skills you would like to explore for your career development.

Works Cited

Arnulf, J. K., Tegner, L., & Larssen, O. (2010). Impression making by résumé layout: Its impact on the probability of being shortlisted. *European Journal of Work and Organizational Psychology, 19*(2), 221–230.

Giddens, A. (1990). *The consequences of modernity*. Stanford University Press.

Burns, G. N., Christiansen, N. D., Morris, M. B., Periard, D. A., & Coaster, J. A. (2014). Effects of applicant personality on resume evaluations. *Journal of Business and Psychology, 29*(4), 573–591.

Calvard, T. (2018). Impostor syndrome as a way of understanding gender and careers. In *Research handbook of diversity and careers* (pp. 211–2226). Edward Elgar Publishing.

Cole, M. S., Feild, H. S., Giles, W. F., & Harris, S. G. (2009). Recruiters' inferences of applicant personality based on resume screening: Do paper people have a personality? *Journal of Business and Psychology, 24*, 5–18.

Dancy, T. E., & Jean-Marie, G. (2014). Faculty of color in higher education: Exploring the intersections of identity, impostorship, and internalized racism. *Mentoring & Tutoring: Partnership in Learning, 22*(4), 354–372.

Horvath, M., & Ryan, A. M. (2003). Antecedents and potential moderators of the relationship between attitudes and hiring discrimination on the basis of sexual orientation. *Sex Roles, 48*, 115–130.

Lazarsfeld, P., & Merton, R. K. (1954). Friendship as a social process: A substantive and methodological analysis. In M. Berger, T. Abel, & H. Charles (Eds.), *Freedom and control in modern society* (Vol. 18 (1), pp. 18–66).

Martins, R., & Anthony, L. (2007). The impostor syndrome: 'What if they find out I don't really belong here?'. In *Stepping stones: A guide for mature aged students at university* (pp. 57–64).

Mishel, E. (2016). Discrimination against queer women in the US workforce: A résumé audit study. *Socius, 2*, 1–13.

Pager, D., Bonikowski, B., & Western, B. (2009). Discrimination in a low-wage labor market: A field experiment. *American Sociological Review, 74*(5), 777–799.

Quillian, L., & Midtbøen, A. H. (2021). Comparative perspectives on racial discrimination in hiring: The rise of field experiments. *Annual Review of Sociology, 47*(1), 391–415.

Stoddard, E., & Pfeifer, G. (2018). *Diversity, equity, and inclusion tools for teamwork: Asset mapping and team processing handbook.* Worcester Polytechnic Institute. Accessed online on Nov. 16, 2021, at https://digital.wpi.edu/concern/generic_works/8w32r8712?locale=en.

Warnock, D. M. (2016). Paradise lost? Patterns and precarity in working-class academic narratives. *Journal of Working-Class Studies, 1*(1), 28–44.

Skills in the Sociology Major

7

When I ask students to name or provide examples of the skills they are developing inside and outside their majors, they look panicked. They are unsure about what I mean by skills or how exactly to describe Sociology as a skills-based major. They think they lack skills. These feelings stem from different, interrelated causes. As previously noted, Sociology students tend to have demographic characteristics linked with underestimating their skills. Faculty may contribute to this anxiety by avoiding the topic. For most faculty, it has been a long time since we were undergraduate students facing the non-academic labor market. Some faculty have never participated in the labor market outside of academia. Because of this lack of current experience, we are not aware of the anxieties and particularities of the job search process. This disconnect between students' needs and their academic mentors' experiences can produce a feeling of disempowerment. If you ask the average professor of Sociology what skills the major offers, the answer will be research skills. For us, this makes sense as we see the main purpose of Sociology as scientific. By contrast, many undergraduate majors care more about the sociological point of view. They feel that claiming to have research skills after taking only the traditional, major core sequence (one Statistics, one Quantitative Methods, and one Qualitative Methods class) makes them a fraud in the eyes of employers. Certain students lack any interest in becoming researchers. You can love Sociology without wanting to become a professor. And while I would argue that research involves a series of complex skills, the term itself is ambiguous and not employer friendly. The word may mean different things to employers within the context of their industries and organizations. They may also have varying degrees of familiarity with a typical Sociology degree.

© The Author(s), under exclusive license to Springer
Nature Switzerland AG 2023
M. A. Martinez, *The Employable Sociologist*,
https://doi.org/10.1007/978-3-031-41323-0_7

The challenge you will face as a Sociology major is two-fold: identify the specific skills you are developing during your studies and articulate them in a language that potential employers understand. While both tasks are unique and will depend on your history and your interests, this chapter will provide guidance in recognizing the kind of skills Sociology majors have developed. We will spend a lot of attention relating sociological skills to skills universally recognized by employers. We will also examine the concept of expertise and examples of how to communicate those skills in the resume. This chapter will concentrate primarily on the Education and Skills section of the resume.

Defining and Identifying Skills

Chapter 6 established the explicit function of the resume as an opportunity to highlight your skills. Now we will define what those are. Using the broadest and most colloquial definition, skills are the ability to do something well. Occupations, jobs, or positions are described in terms of specific skill combinations. You can find categories and lists of skills in books and on the Internet; there are no standards controlling their use. Punctuality, for example, can be both a skill (the ability to arrive on time on a regular basis) or a character trait. For resumes, I have found it useful to distinguish between three types of skills: Technical, Transferable, and Socioemotional.

Technical Skills

Technical skills are the easiest to identify. They are usually associated with certifications even if you learned them outside of formal classes or courses. The narrow definition is the capacity to use software packages or systems. Technical skills that rely heavily on software, even when the skill goes beyond them, should include both the skill and the software used. For example, Photography or Social Media Marketing are technical skills, but you should always mention which software or platform you utilize. Photography should include Photoshop or Invicto, and Graphic Design might be Canva or Adobe Creative Suite. Social Media Marketing may include Facebook, LinkedIn, Instagram, TikTok, etc. Providing the details adds credibility. Table 7.1 offers a list of software most commonly used by Sociology students inside and outside the major.

Technical skills go beyond familiarity with software. Sociology majors can claim research skills either as technical or transferable skills. While methodologies

Defining and Identifying Skills

Table 7.1 Software Commonly Used by Sociology Students

Statistics	Design	Business	Website Design
SPSS	Adobe Creative Suite: Photoshop, Illustrator, InDesign, Premiere Pro, Acrobat	Microsoft Office Suite: Word, Excel, PowerPoint	Dreamweaver
SAS	Canva	Google Suite: Gmail, Drive, Calendar, Meet, Docs, Sheets, Slides	WordPress
Stata	inPixio (Photography)	Salesforce (Point of Sale)	Squarespace
R	Prezi		
MATLAB			

tend to be specific in nature (technical), they can also be applied to a variety of environments and situations (transferable). Research, or even Qualitative or Quantitative Research, suggests a transferable skill. These general categories describe a way of thinking rather than mastery of specific methodologies. Most Sociology curricula include one Statistics class, one Quantitative Methodology class, and one Qualitative Methodology class. Mentioning these classes in fact signals educational quality and rigor. But most employers will have no idea that the Sociology curriculum includes "math" or that many students avoid Sociology precisely because they do not want to take our rigorous core classes. If you are considering a position that involves research in any of its forms, mentioning core classes may not be enough. The key to claiming research as a technical skill is to be specific about the methodology you have mastered. Table 7.2 lists specific methodologies. Methodologies have different names depending on the context of the research and the field of study. For example, oral histories and interviews are, from a skills perspective, the same, but carry different names. Use the language of the job posting to name your skills, even if you learned them under a different name. We will talk more about how to emphasize technical research skills in the Education and Skills section of the resume later in the chapter.

Sociology students may learn other technical skills in their major and in their non-Sociology classes. Some faculty design classes to be more experiential or to provide more practical training. Consider the examples of Writing and Communication skills. Normally, sociologists do considerable writing, a transferable skill. But Creative Writing, Social Media Writing, Public Relations and Advertising

Table 7.2 Research Skills/Methodologies

Observational Study	Survey Research
Focus Group	Descriptive Research
Interview	Experimental Research
Content Analysis	Causal Research
Discourse Analysis	Correlation Research
Grounded Theory	Regression Analysis
Ethnography	Data Analytics/Biostatistics/Econometrics/Modeling
Action Research	Program Assessment
Narrative Research	Media Analysis
Phenomenology	Case Study
Historical or Archival Research	Bibliographic Research
Oral History	Participant Observation

Writing, are specialized enough to be considered technical (even if the term Technical Writing is used to describe communications in technical fields like engineering and medicine). Communication, also a general skill, assumes greater stature and significance when you are more specific, differentiating between Intercultural Communication, Media Communication, Interpersonal Communication, or Marketing Communication. To provide evidence of your technical skills, list relevant class projects, jobs, or extracurricular activities in your resume. You do not need a certification to demonstrate competency, although taking the time and effort to get one carries weight.

Mastery of Modern Languages is another important technical skill. Most universities require one year or more of college-level language. A few students continue their language education beyond this requirement, even combining their Sociology major with other formal credentials. Some students come from immigrant households and are bilingual. Depending on their importance for the job application, language skills might deserve their own section heading or may go in the general skills section. They can be placed first or elsewhere in the resume.

Students often omit their language skills, whether out of insecurity about their proficiency, fear of ethnic bias, or because it does not appear in most job descriptions. In my experience, when students are forced to use their language skills, they tend to be more proficient than their self-evaluations indicate. The quantity and variety of jobs requiring foreign language skills continues to increase as many organizations and teams become increasingly multicultural and international. Your language skills, however acquired, can provide an advantage over other candidates. While it is true that not all jobs require a second language, these skills signal intellectual curiosity and multicultural competencies.

The Interagency Language Roundtable (ILR) developed the most common standard used to describe proficiency levels in a language. It divides proficiency into six levels, 0–5 (see Table 7.3). The system can be problematic because it combines proficiency in Reading, Writing, and Speaking into a single level, which may not accurately reflect an individual's proficiency. When students raise these concerns, I recommend separating proficiency into three different dimensions: Reading, Writing, and Speaking. Each is a separate skill, and proficiency can range from Basic, Intermediate, or Advanced. Basic levels usually are equivalent to one college year of language training for most European languages. For languages that are linguistically and culturally unrelated to English like Mandarin, Japanese, or Russian, it may take two years to achieve Basic proficiency. Intermediate level is usually the equivalent of two years of college language training. Advanced proficiency requires vocabulary appropriate for a larger variety of contexts and topics, as well as more complex writing and reading. I would usually measure advanced proficiency as the ability to take a substantive class (think literature or social sciences) and do public presentations in the language. I recommend using this guide as a starting point, and adjusting your level accordingly. Usually, reading and writing skill levels tend to be more closely linked than speaking, depending on the source of your language training. For example, students who learn language skills at home may have a much higher proficiency in speaking than reading and writing. Students who read complex literary works may not be able to have a simple conversation in the language. The European Centre for Modern Languages, part of the Council of Europe, has created a useful tool for self-evaluating your language skills: https://edl.ecml.at/LanguageFun/Self-evaluateyourlanguageskills!/tabid/2194/Default.aspx

If you are Intermediate level or above, take a certification test. Include the level and certifying organization on your resume. Although these tests tend to charge a fee, they are worth the investment for the third-person evidence of proficiency they

Table 7.3 Interagency Language Roundtable (ILR) Scale

ILR Scale	
Level	Label
0	No Proficiency
1	Elementary Proficiency
2	Limited Working Proficiency
3	General Professional Proficiency
4	Advanced Professional Proficiency
5	Functionally Native Professional Proficiency

provide and the advantage they can give you over other candidates who don't have certification.

A final level of language skill is bilingualism, or native proficiency in two languages. Bilingualism does not mean perfection; even those whose only language is English, for example, may not always use correct vocabulary or grammar. While I consider languages a technical skill at any level, the specific job position associated with these skills is in the area of translation. To claim skills in either written or simultaneous translation requires certification or experience. Volunteering or work experience are ways to gain such experience.

Transferable Skills, NACE Competencies, and Sociology
Transferable skills are usually more general and applicable to a variety of contexts, positions, and tasks. Because of their general nature, they may sound vague or "empty." Universities and employers have created a common language to recognize and describe transferable skills, particularly for majors without defined career paths unrelated to Managerial Sciences. The National Association of Colleges and Employers (NACE), which provides a point of contact between Career Center professionals in universities and Human Resources in organizations, developed the following categories to identify competencies (transferable skills and competencies are synonymous).

- Critical Thinking/Problem Solving
- Oral/Written Communications
- Teamwork/Collaboration
- Digital Technology
- Leadership
- Professionalism and Work Ethic
- Global/Intercultural Fluency
- Career Management

Ironically, faculty and students in the Humanities and Social Sciences are often unaware of these competencies, which they in fact possess in abundance. I would argue that a well-constructed Sociology curriculum develops all of these skills. Table 7.4 names and describes each competency as developed by NACE and lists the corresponding activities and learning outcomes that students acquire through the typical Sociology curriculum:

This table serves as a sort of dictionary, matching sociological and managerial-based concepts that you can easily reference. The first column shows the type of competency and its description taken verbatim from NACE. This is the language that employers expect you to use when describing competencies/transferable skills. While we Sociology faculty are obsessed with research, research, research, and are

Table 7.4 NACE Competencies and their Sociological Equivalents

NACE Competencies		Methodology Competencies *Ciabattari et al. (2018)*	Expanded Competencies
Critical Thinking & Problem Solving	Exercise sound reasoning to analyze issues, make decisions, and overcome problems. The individual is able to obtain, interpret, and use knowledge, facts, and data in this process and may demonstrate originality and inventiveness.	• Make an evidence-based argument • Evaluate strengths and weaknesses of different research methods • Create hypotheses • Interpret results of different types of data gathering	• Evaluate biases in sources and people • Identify negative consequences of behaviors, norms, procedures, and laws • Make connections between individual behaviors, problems and issues, and broader social systems • Identify how specific systems reinforce inequality among people of different races, genders, ethnicities, sexual orientations, and classes

(continued)

Table 7.4 (continued)

NACE Competencies		Methodology Competencies *Ciabattari et al. (2018)*	Expanded Competencies
Oral & Written Communication	Articulate thoughts and ideas clearly and effectively in written and oral forms to persons inside and outside of the organization. The individual has public speaking skills, is able to express ideas to others, and can write/edit memos, letters, and complex technical reports clearly and effectively.	• Write a report that can be understood by non-sociologists • Make presentations using software such as PowerPoint, Prezi, or other computer programs • Describe percentages and statistics in a bivariate table • Graphically display data • Write research or grant proposals	• Write a report describing a social system, issue, topic, or problem for a general audience • Use language that empowers people and avoid language that discriminates, marginalizes, or offends them
Teamwork & Collaboration	Build collaborative relationships with colleagues and customers representing diverse cultures, races, ages, genders, religions, lifestyles, and viewpoints. The individual is able to work within a team structure and can negotiate and manage conflict.	• Work with people who differ in race, ethnicity, gender, or class	• Use sociological knowledge to help other people achieve their organizational, career, and personal goals • Develop collaborative relationships with individuals of diverse backgrounds to achieve organizational, career, and personal goals

(continued)

Table 7.4 (continued)

NACE Competencies		Methodology Competencies *Ciabattari et al. (2018)*	Expanded Competencies
Digital Technology	Leverage existing digital technologies ethically and efficiently to solve problems, complete tasks, and accomplish goals. The individual demonstrates effective adaptability to new and emerging technologies.	• Analyze data with statistical packages • Use qualitative data analysis packages • Use computers to find information to develop a bibliography or a list of references	
Leadership	Leverage the strengths of others to achieve common goals and use interpersonal skills to coach and develop others. The individual is able to assess and manage his or her own emotions and those of others, use empathetic skills to guide and motivate, and organize, prioritize, and delegate work.		• Use sociological knowledge to propose alternatives or create new processes and systems • Use understanding of socialization and stratification processes to promote equality of opportunity • Use sociological knowledge to develop and promote empathy for those who are different

(continued)

Table 7.4 (continued)

NACE Competencies		Methodology Competencies Ciabattari et al. (2018)	Expanded Competencies
Professionalism & Work Ethic	Demonstrate personal accountability and effective work habits, such as punctuality, working productively with others, and time workload management, and understand the impact of nonverbal communication on professional work image. The individual demonstrates integrity and ethical behavior, acts responsibly with the interests of the larger community in mind, and is able to learn from his or her own mistakes.	• Identify ethical issues in sociological research	• Behave in ways that minimize harm to others and maximize larger social benefits • Evaluate the fit between personal values, interests, personality preferences, and particular organizational contexts and work conditions • Recommend specific changes in behaviors, norms, procedures, laws, and systems to increase positive collaboration in multicultural teams
Intercultural Fluency	Value, respect, and learn from diverse cultures, races, ages, genders, sexual orientations, and religions. The individual demonstrates openness, inclusiveness, sensitivity, and the ability to interact respectfully with all people and understand individual differences.	• Work with people who differ in race, ethnicity, gender, or class	• Understand and explain how the experiences of different groups may affect behavior and emotions • Understand how historical events may affect people's current perceptions, particularly for those outside the US and Western Europe

absolutely convinced of its uses in the outside world in a variety of industries and positions, we seldom provide specific examples to show how our work is applicable in the workplace. The second column provides equivalencies between the different research tasks performed in Sociology classes and the competencies developed by NACE. Any of your class projects or experiences in the research process becomes a potential example of a particular competency.

Despite faculty's fixation on research, limiting the transferable skills developed by Sociology to our research methods is selling the discipline short. Sociological theories and knowledge provide a range of specific skills or competencies. The third column provides examples of typical competency/transferable skills developed through thematic classes. In this column, you will find content familiar from Sociology classes, but expressed in terms of the potential actions they create. The thinking versus action orientation is a key difference between the language of Sociology and that of the Managerial Sciences typically used by employers. When writing your resume, keep in mind that knowing how to think about something provides you with the capacity to act on it. We will talk more about the language of the resume in Chap. 8.

Socioemotional Skills

Socioemotional skills can be the most vague and controversial type of skill. The intellectual source of these skills is Child Psychology, and it refers to the development of self-control, or the ability to regulate one's thoughts, emotions, and behaviors. Socioemotional skills are associated with the work done in Psychology on Emotional Intelligence (Gardner, 2011). Socioemotional skills are also associated with personality traits, and are a positive and accepted way to describe your internal dispositions. While few people want to admit having high neuroticism, you can frame it in positive terms like "diligent" and "responsible." The fundamental concept is that all tasks, and therefore all transferable and technical skills, require a pre-existing foundational disposition. Since employers are going to make assumptions about your personality based on your resume regardless, why not "guide" their impressions of you by including selective socioemotional skills in your Skills Section? But don't forget that since it is important to both "show" and tell, you may want to include activities in other parts of the resume that support your claims of a particular socioemotional skill. For example, mentioning a high GPA is evidence of reliability and responsibility. Table 7.5 provides a list of resume-relevant socioemotional skills. However, the best source for the specific words to use will be in the job posting and the company's website. Mirror the language of the organization and remember that search engines and most personnel professionals will really be hunting for keywords in resumes.

Table 7.5 Socioemotional Skills

Teamwork-Oriented	Adaptable
Goal-Oriented	Passionate
Customer-Oriented	Self-Motivated
Relationship Builder	Positive
Organized	Proactive Listener
Calm or Patient	Decisive
Creative	Reliable
Realistic or Pragmatic	Optimistic
Collaborative	

Another recommendation is not to get too hung up over the analytical differences between skills. I included this typology because as sociologists we often understand things best by putting them in boxes. While I separate these three types into analytically independent categories, the lines between them are arbitrary. Skills develop as bundles or packages of abilities. For example, learning to do quantitative data analysis means acquiring the technical skill to run different statistical models in a particular software package. But such work leads you to develop the transferable skills involved in connecting data to behaviors that transcend any software. And while learning how to run models requires an attention to detail, dealing with the realities of data cleaning and modeling also improves that skill. Always articulate your skills in the format or language used in the job postings and in ways that maximize their visibility within the resume.

Expertise and Sociology

Discussed less often in the context of career development is the opportunity the resume also offers to display your expertise in relation to the working of an organization. We usually call this expertise "business knowledge." The university world confers official recognition of expertise when you complete a thesis or a dissertation in an area of knowledge. Academics also assume you have expertise if you obtain a terminal degree in that area. In the work world, the barriers for claiming expertise are lower and less defined. You can determine your right to claim expertise by answering the question, Do I know more than most other people about the topic? Claims to expertise are stronger if you can demonstrate both experience (personal or professional) and academic knowledge in the topic. Knowledge does not require a degree, but only a few classes in the topic. Two important types of expertise are:

1. **Industry/Business Expertise.** Claims to expertise in a particular industry can be based on college classes related to that area or work or extensive volunteering experience. If you took classes on law and society or criminology, for

instance, you could claim expertise on institutions and organizations related to the criminal justice system. If you took classes on marketing and consumption, you could claim expertise in consumer behavior. Sociology of education provides direct expertise on educational institutions. Another way to claim expertise is through your hobbies. For example, if gourmet baking is a hobby, that might provide certain knowledge of the food and baking industries. The same applies to music, sports, arts, environmental issues, and numerous others. America is one of those unique places where people can make a living in industries related to their passions and individual experiences.

2. **Population Expertise.** This type of expertise claims knowledge of a particular population in a specific role or setting. Perhaps you have worked at Gap and feel that you know consumer behavior patterns of women in their 40s and 50s. Or maybe you have worked with toddlers or preschoolers. That experience combined with training and two or three related college classes (such as in Child Psychology), can allow you to claim expertise in Early Child Development without necessarily needing a major or a minor in the subject. There are cases in which intense life experiences can also qualify as an expertise. Take the case of one of my older students. She had a severely autistic son and had to postpone starting her degree for a long time because her priority was to provide the best care and resources for him. She can easily claim to be an expert on autism's impact on children and their parents, as well as the challenges and resources available for both populations.

Do be careful about claiming expertise related to a marginalized or vulnerable group that you are not part of unless you have strong academic credentials or extensive interpersonal experience. A one-week service trip to a rural community in Nicaragua does not create expertise on Nicaraguans or Latinos. Be sure to include those trips in your resume as evidence of your interest in particular communities, but this should be communicated with nuance.

Expressing Your Sociological "Self"

Where do you express your sociological self in the resume? The first place is in the Education section. In addition to your major, university information, and expected or actual graduation date, you can add a small subsection on relevant classes taken. What classes are relevant? Those that show familiarity with the language (and spirit) of the requirements of the job you are seeking. This should be one of the most flexible sections in your resume, modified to fit the job posting. Do not waste valuable space listing classes that may be too obvious or redundant, like Introduction to Sociology or Sociological Theory. In addition to theory and methodology classes, most Sociology programs include electives that allow students to pursue their own interests in greater depth. They also may offer a set of specialty classes concentrated in distinct areas of Sociology, such as Gender and Race, Stratification, Organizational Studies, Demography, Social Psychology, Medical Sociology, and Political Sociology, among others. The American Sociological Association website provides a long list of the types of Sociology offered by colleges across the country in its Sections page at https://www.asanet.org/communities-sections/sections/current-sections.

While your major is important, it is not the only thing that matters about your education. Do not restrict yourself to classes in Sociology; anything you have taken in your minor, general education, or electives can be mentioned as relevant classes. Think of your classes as cards in a deck; choose the best card(s) for each application. A list of classes can help you define and project your action orientation. For example, if you consider yourself a communicator, you can add classes like Sociology of Media, Public Speaking, or Sociology of Communication. If you want to emphasize an organizer profile, classes like Organizational Studies, Network Theory, or Sociology of Entrepreneurship could work. In addition to action profiles, a Relevant Classes section can express industry or population expertise. Sociology of Education or Sociology of Technology can convey knowledge of those industries. Race and Ethnicity or Gender and Society can support claims to Intercultural Fluency and Ethical Behavior, demonstrating tolerance and anti-discrimination.

You can also display your sociological self through examples of your work. Adding titles or descriptions of projects performed during your studies in the Education section can show knowledge of specific methodologies and expertise. The following are examples of projects done by Sociology students in their research and capstone classes:

- Observational Study of the Relationship between Parenting Style and Child Temperament
- Ethnographic Study of Identity Formation in Environmental Social Movements
- Survey Analysis of Students' Attitudes about Social Media Platforms
- Correlational Study of Food Availability and Happiness: Global Perspective
- Regression Analysis of Social Capital Determinants among US Adults
- Visual Analysis of Instagram Posts Portraying Masculinity
- Authentically Depressed: Interview Study of the Social Status of Depressed Identity on Reddit Forums
- Oral History of Latino Students and their Experiences of Discrimination in the Educational System
- Survey Assessment of Major Satisfaction among Recent Sociology Graduates

Conferences and poster presentations also belong in the Education section. Just like class projects, their titles reflect skills and expertise. Their presence on your resume also can indicate communication or design skills. Instead of putting these projects in the Education section, you might create a separate section of Research Projects, like Gina did in Fig. 6.2. That will let you provide more detail about your research experience.

The Education section should include all academic awards, group and Honors Society memberships, extracurricular activities, and your GPA. Remember, these elements support your claims of skills and expertise, as well as your interest and ability to learn in those areas. Almost any group membership and extracurricular activity is associated with certain skills and expertise. For example, if you participate in a theater, music, or an arts group, you can claim creativity in addition to any technical skills developed through those activities. If you play sports, you can claim to be collaborative and teamwork-oriented. Students gain social media skills promoting their clubs. Even gardening, the most seemingly unrelated activity to most jobs, can reflect patience and attention to detail. All extracurricular activities are related to industries or markets where you will have expert knowledge.

If you are hunting for a job after graduation, you only need to include information about the BA degree you are pursuing. Only include high school information on a resume drafted during your first year of university. A final note on the Education section relates to the GPA. While there is no real research on the exact meaning of different GPAs for employers beyond "the higher the better," at least one academic article recommends omitting any GPA lower than 3.0. Some Career Centers recommend only including your GPA if it is 3.5 or higher.

Creating Your Skills Section in the Resume

If you have done your work in the Education, Work Experience, and Extracurricular sections on your resume, then creating a Skills section should be easy. This is the only slightly redundant component of your resume, the part where you can *tell* what other elements in your resume have tried to *show*. This section should be placed prominently in your resume, either at the beginning, the left column, or the end. It should always include *all* your technical skills, regardless of the posted job description. You never know what kind of competitive advantage such skills might give you. Students of color tend to forget to include their language skills, either because they do not feel comfortable with their proficiency or they do not think of them as skills. In the case of transferable skills, you should include everything in which you have a certification, award, class, significant work, or extracurricular experience. Finally, I recommend compiling a list of socioemotional skills that you can rotate in or out of your resume depending on the job you are seeking. Include a maximum of two of those skills at a time, listed in the order of their relevance to your desired job.

Conclusion

Undergraduate majors develop multiple transferable skills during their studies within and outside the discipline. Skills, at the most basic level, are the capacity to do something. They can be categorized as technical, transferable, and socioemotional. To present you with an advantage in the job search process, you must articulate them in the language of business and the employer. The list of competencies created by the National Association of Colleges and Employers offers a good framework for matching sociological transferable skills to that language. The most common technical skills among sociologists are software and second language proficiency. Socioemotional skills can be included in the Skills section of the resume in moderation, giving priority to your technical and transferable skills. Expertise in industries or populations can also be highlighted. Organize and adjust your resume to fit the requirements and the description of the job you are pursuing.

Discussion Questions

1. How confident do you feel about the quality of the Sociology major compared to other majors? What are the reasons for this level of confidence? Is there anything you can do to increase your confidence?
2. Talk with other sociologists about your language skills. Are there any common narratives? What is their assessment of your skill level?
3. How do you feel about research (academic, government, or private) as a potential career path?
4. What is the most common skills profile of Sociology students? What is the main strength of this profile or its major weakness?
5. Does knowing something about a topic make you more likely to make good decisions on related problems? Why or why not?
6. Is it possible to develop Socioemotional skills or are they really set personality traits?
7. Can you think of additional Socioemotional skills beyond those mentioned in Table 7.5?

Action/Reflection Activity

1. Make a list of activities you participated in in high school. Using the tables in this chapter, determine the skills and expertise that each activity highlights or developed.
2. Make a list of the Sociology classes you have taken and the skills and expertise associated with those classes.
3. Make a list of the titles of all the final or major projects you have done in your Sociology classes. Select three examples that you consider the most meaningful or relevant to the kind of position or industry you are considering for the future. How can you name them to display your skills and expertise?
4. Request or print an unofficial copy of your transcript (or find a complete list of your classes outside the major). Consulting the tables in this chapter, determine the skills associated with them. It might be useful to review the learning objectives of the classes from each syllabus.
5. Make a list of all your extracurricular activities as a college student. Use the tables in this chapter to determine the skills and expertise developed or displayed by those activities.
6. Think of your contributions to your family, hobbies, or other regular activities. Use the tables in this chapter to identify the skills and expertise developed or showcased by those activities.
7. Using the information in Chaps. 6 and 7, create the Education section of your resume.
8. Using the information collected during this activity, create a list of primary skills (technical, transferable, and socioemotional) and expertise for the Skills section of your resume. Create a list of "secondary" skills or expertise that you can add or omit depending on the nature of the job or industry in question.
9. Thinking of your skills, are there any jobs for which you are qualified? Are there any skills that you need to develop for the job you want?

Works Cited

Gardner, H. E. (2011). *Frames of mind: The theory of multiple intelligences*. Basic Books.

The Language of Business 8

Work Experience and Extracurriculars are key elements of a resume; they let you present evidence showing that you have the right skills for the job. Experiences outside of academia and paid jobs also demonstrate potential for future skill development, as well as passion. Sociology students face three main issues when dealing with the Work Experience section. First, many feel that they have no experience at all because they have not done paid work. Second, they feel that their experiences are not relevant to the jobs they want. Finally, they struggle to translate what they have done into words that "speak" to potential employers. Sociology and Human Resources have content in common, but their languages are distinctly different.

The first two problems are related. In my experience, all Sociology students have work experience, although sometimes they do not recognize it. Part of the issue is related to how society defines work. Many activities that should be compensated are requested for free under the excuse that they are "learning experiences." Just in case there is confusion, any activity fulfilling at least one of the following conditions can be included in the Work Experience section of your resume:

- Got paid, it is a job.
- Should have gotten paid, it is a job.
- Was an internship providing bona fide experience in a position, it is a job.
- Had serious responsibilities that other people depended on for a significant period of time, it is a job.
- Were a Teaching Assistant or Research Assistant for more than three months and you did significant work but were not paid, it is a job.
- Were self-employed and made money, it is a job.

Internships are a common source of work experience. In an ideal world, every Sociology junior or senior has been involved in an internship. Also ideally, the internship is in a position, organization, or industry that interests them. Finally, in a fair world, that position would be paid. Rarely are those conditions met, however. Still, students should seek out internships. For short-term experiences (six months or less), any internship is better than no internship. That said, I would not recommend staying in a position more than six months if you are not getting paid or if the position does not fit your interests. Organizations sometimes use students as sources of free labor longer than they should. It is unlikely that you will ever have a future in that organization if they have kept you in an unpaid or low-level position for too long.

For students who already know or think they know what career they want, an internship offers a leg up in relevant experience and an opportunity to evaluate whether their expectations match reality. Students who are undecided about their careers also benefit by getting to explore and then choose or discard a particular path. Sometimes the only way to know if a career path fits your personal goals is through experience. Beyond their educational and experiential advantages, internships give you content for your Work Experience section of the resume. I recommend that all students start exploring internship opportunities late in their freshman year and begin applying early in their sophomore year or equivalent credit hours. Plan to do two or three internships while in school.

With many internships currently unpaid, you may not be able to afford to engage in one internship, let alone three. You may need a job to pay for your studies and living expenses. I can understand the need to keep student loans to a minimum. If that describes your situation, you may question the value of including an entry-level, low-prestige, paid job on your resume. *Always* include all jobs, regardless of the level or quality of the work. I have helped students describe their activities as a barista, sales associate, receptionist, peer mentor, and customer service representative. Relevant work experience is better, but in its absence other work experiences can show evidence of key transferable skills. Many of these skills complement those you develop in your major. Some jobs are associated with specific skills or expertise while others can be framed in more diverse ways. For example, if you worked as a barista, you could emphasize your communication skills, your attention to detail, or your ability to multitask. For a different interpretation, you can focus on conflict resolution or your expertise in areas of the coffee or hospitality industries. Almost any job provides opportunities to demonstrate critical thinking or leadership skills. Everything depends on how you frame the experience. Potential employers tend to respond well to the right framing. It reflects effective communication skills.

Before starting the Work Experience section, make a list of all your experiences, no matter how unrelated you think they are to your job aspirations. First, attach any technical skills learned, even at a basic level. Then, using the NACE competency and socioemotional skills tables shown in the previous chapter, assign skills to each position. Think about the kind of jobs and industries you want to target. Look at postings of related positions. Then design your Work Experience section to reflect the specific description of your target job. Just as with the Education and Skills sections, you may have different versions of Work Experience. I recommend preparing descriptions of all the jobs you have had, regardless of their nature. When crafting your descriptions, you need to consider the accepted cultural elements of business communication. Sociologists call these norms biases.

Biases in the Language of Business

The language of most organizations is that of Management Science, which itself is the embodiment of capitalist culture. Its influence permeates even nonprofit and government institutions. This culture takes knowledge developed by the Social Sciences and the Humanities and tailors it to fulfill the goals of the organization. Yet, the language of management differs in considerable ways from that used in Sociology. The third part of this book will provide an in-depth view of managerial culture and its consequences for your career development. For now, we will concentrate on the language differences relevant to the application process. The two main language biases in the job application process are positive framing and action orientation.

Positive Framing

Positive framing is an essential element of the application process. Employers expect you to show them your best self, and the application materials and processes are a test of how you respond to that challenge. Positive framing is also important because it is embedded in communication functions within the organization, including communications with stakeholders like investors, customers, communities, and employees. Companies use positive framing to help structure their relationships with their stakeholders. They avoid projecting a lack of control or communicating negative events and they seldom admit problems. The best example is one from my personal experience. Prior to my academic career, I worked as an advisor in a Mexican Business School. My boss insisted that there were no problems, only areas of opportunity. He is one of the main reasons I became a sociologist: I wanted to be able to argue that there *were* problems and that we should face them head on. As you know, social problems are an important aspect of Sociology, so a no-problems approach can require some adjusting. For your own professional career, a positive framing bias means that the language you use in your sociological studies is full of minefields. Concepts such as alienation, exploitation, and domination carry negative connotations. Most sociologists would use the term racism without a second thought, but in the outside world it is considered problematic and accusatory. The business world prefers softer, more neutral terms; instead of racism, they might say racial bias or simply bias.

The use of positive terms is relevant to the Education, Work Experience, and Extracurricular/Other Experience sections. For Education, you have the option of modifying your class and project titles to fit the target audience. Management Science has done an excellent job of providing positive (or neutral) framing for theories dealing with negative social phenomena. For example, while we talk about alienation, they examine increased autonomy, meaning, and connection to work. Thus, rather than talk about a paper in terms of reducing alienation or levels of alienation, you can modify the description to the more neutral "levels of autonomy." If the organization or the job posting clearly states a social problem, which is often the case for nonprofits, there is no need to modify the language of your classes and projects. You can also decide not to change anything if you feel that any organization that disapproves of "critical" language is not the place for you. For the Work Experience and Extracurricular sections, the changes would apply only to your descriptions of job activities and should be limited to neutral verbs without negative connotations. For example, use "improve" rather than "fix," as fixing something implies something was wrong. Saying "needs fixing" can be seen as criticizing clients, fellow employees, or organizations. While negative language is less likely to surface in the context of extracurriculars, the same principle applies.

Action Orientation

The second bias, that toward action, is fundamental in how you treat the Work Experience section of your resume and in your transition from school to work in general. While your education has focused on learning how to think, getting a job depends on demonstrating your ability to act and determine courses of action. Academia gives you the time and space to think about a problem from myriad perspectives. You have time to decompose its nature and consequences. If you have ever been in a faculty meeting, you may know that we can spend more than a decade talking about a problem without acting to resolve it. By contrast, managerial culture emphasizes doing and acting, if not as fast as possible, at least before the problem grows worse.

How does this orientation affect the language? One of the assumptions of Managerial Science is that if you use the language of actions, then you will be more likely to act. For job descriptions, it means starting each sentence with a verb. Now we can have endless discussions about whether this assumption is true, and Sociology has strong literature on decoupling which explores how the use of language may be divorced from actual organizational behaviors (Meyer & Rowan, 1977). For the job application, however, your capacity for action will be judged by your use of verbs. The next section of this chapter will show you how to describe activities performed in jobs to reflect your capacity for action.

Job Description, Skills, and Action Orientation

Recalling the resume elements discussed in Chap. 6, a simple but effective format for presenting job descriptions is shown below. Remember that the Work Experience section must include your role, the company, general location of activities, dates of employment, activity descriptions, and achievements (if possible). The role you performed should get the most emphasis. Sometimes students mistakenly emphasize the company rather than their role. The function of the resume is to provide evidence of your skills, which are shown through your role, rather than the organization's. You can emphasize the position by setting it off in bold or uppercase text. You can write the name of the organization in Italics. In one exception to this order, I would recommend emphasizing the organization itself *if* that would better fit the job posting. For example, the organization you worked for may offer expertise within the business or industry you are trying to enter.

> **Sales Associate** | Candyality | Sunnydale, IL September 2018–Present
> - Engaged with customers in a fast-paced retail setting, providing excellent front of house support
> - Responsibilities include merchandising, customer service, operating multiple POS systems, and general upkeep of the store
> - Assisted in community Halloween event in Southport Corridor in Lakeview and helped prepare supplies for a 5k run sponsored by Candyality

The format of the information is very good, but the wording of the description could be improved by correcting the following:

Inconsistencies in grammatical forms. The first and third bullet points start with verbs in the past tense (as recommended), but the second sentence starts with a noun and is written in present tense.

Use of at least one empty adjective (excellent).

Redundancy and excessive detail. You don't need to mention Candyality in both the title and the description. Sentences have extra words not needed to describe the activity.

Lists no achievements.

Low-Quality Verbs (Assist, Providing, Helped)

I have found that the quality of verbs seems to be particularly troublesome for my students. English language speakers prefer the simplest word to reference something. While acceptable in daily speech, the resume's language must be more precise and memorable. Remember, your goal is to show that you have a skill. Avoiding empty or overly general verbs like those listed below will elevate the descriptive power of your language:

- Do
- Make
- Assist
- Help
- Perform

These verbs fail to adequately describe the activity. They also make you sound insecure. Help and assist sound like you do not feel capable of performing the task on your own. Organizations know that you will have a boss, and that a lot of work is done in teams with a coordinator. It is not necessary to indicate that you worked under someone's supervision. And although you should always search for more exact verbs, sometimes you will get stuck needing the low-quality ones. That is okay. Just try not to depend on them as crutches instead of looking for better alternatives.

Choose verbs that fit the skill(s) you want to showcase. For example, most people would naturally favor "made" instead of "constructed." These words may seem similar, but made is an ambiguous description of the skill. Constructed implies more careful (or critical) thinking and actual manual labor. In contrast to constructed, "designed" emphasizes more of the thinking and less of the physical work of doing. Below you can find a better version of the original description.

> **Sales Associate** | Candyality | Sunnydale, IL September 2018–Present
> - Engaged with customers in a fast-paced retail setting
> - Promoted sales, operated multiple POS systems, and arranged displays to maximize appeal
> - Organized promotional community events
> - Obtained recognition as best sales associate three months in a row

If you compare both descriptions, the new version is more direct and efficient, and says more in fewer words. Distracting details have been deleted and an achievement sentence added. Writing in this new way takes practice, but you can call on friends and family or your university Career Center for help. In order to make verb selection easier, the next section of this chapter will offer job descriptions for specific positions and skills. I selected these examples for their high quality and with an eye toward the types of jobs I see most often on Sociology students' resumes. The jobs are organized by position type and include retail, hospitality, communication, education, fundraising and canvassing, and research categories. These position descriptions normally encompass more than one NACE competency or socioemotional skill. They include activities that can be used in the Work Experiences and Extracurriculars/Other Experience/Volunteer Experience sections. Use them as starting points to describe your own experiences.

Retail Jobs

Many students work in retail jobs to fund or supplement their income. These jobs do not pay well or may be based on commission. Students still prefer them for their often flexible hours and because they fit the school year calendar. What students tend to underestimate is how well these jobs speak to their communication and teamwork skills. Anybody who can last more than a couple of months in the customer service industry demonstrates the resilience and patience of a saint. Let us review three examples describing this type of job.

Buyer/Seller | Plato's Closet | Sunnydale, IL August 2019–Present

- Sorted items, determined value, and generated a quote based on style, brand, condition, and age
- Managed Instagram store account, posting latest trends, styles, and visual design
- Trained new hires to learn store operations, such as back-stocking, floor organization and layout, display design, register operations, and customer service
- Increased Instagram followers by 15%
- Attained a personal average dollar sale 35% higher than store average

This is the best, most-focused description of a retail job I have ever seen. It is very complete and it details achievements in two areas of activity. Skills associated with this description include social media communication, training (education), leadership, supervision, and customer service. The description also uses verbs effectively. Obviously, the person had a valuable experience in this job and was able to describe the skills developed very well. Other workers in similar positions may have had a different experience. See the following good but less rich description of another retail job experience.

Beauty Advisor | Ulta Beauty | Sunnydale, IL December 2020–Present

- Built and deepened productive and positive customer relations with high-quality service and a focus on gaining loyalty
- Capitalized on upselling opportunities for additional products and services to increase sales
- Advised customers on product quality, located specific products, and answered broad questions

Although less detailed than the Buyer/Seller example, this Beauty Advisor description reflects communication skills, goal orientation, and critical thinking.

Hospitality Jobs

Students take hospitality jobs for reasons similar to those in retail: the flexible hours and compatible seasonality. With its questionable working conditions and

Low-Quality Verbs (Assist, Providing, Helped) 125

wage practices, this is a difficult industry and not one commonly sought by Sociology students for long-term careers. In other words, this industry is an area that could benefit from the transformational impact of sociological thinking. Although the tasks tend to be mechanic, do not underestimate their potential to lead you to good jobs or to develop demonstrable skills. Often difficult by nature, these jobs represent a "badge of honor" for those who see them through. Employers know that they entail handling demanding situations and people. That brings us to the potential framing of the hospitality jobs of barista and waiter.

Barista/Server | Joe Donut | Sunnydale, IL January 2017–March 2020
- Expedited customer orders with accuracy while managing interruptions
- Provided personalized hospitality and customer service
- Determined and maintained ideal supply levels to meet physical demands

This example provides evidence of expertise in the coffee and casual restaurant industries. In this case, the student had a passion for social justice and coffee which came together in a job for a fair-trade organization. The experience also translates into effective communication skills by being able to detect what people want and need through interaction. While not mentioned in the NACE competencies, Customer Service of any kind is a skill that is both transferable and technical involving a complex set of communication activities. The student could also claim good organizational skills, evidenced through the following and adapting of procedures. Organizational skills are basically a combination of critical thinking and the socio-emotional skill of attention to detail. The description also provides a sense of efficiency and good time-management. Furthermore, more than three years holding a customer service job indicates that this person is responsible, stable, resilient, and persistent. You can "sell" the same experience from different angles.

Waiter | Zizi's Cafe | Sunnydale, IL May–September 2019, 2020
- Built positive connections with customers through expedient service and positive attitude
- Enabled customers to make decisions based on taste and interest by sharing knowledge of menu
- Greeted new customers, discussed specials, took drink and food orders
- Increased efficiency by organizing, stocking, and cleaning server areas
- Performed opening, closing, and shift change duties

While the jobs of waiter and barista are very similar, the descriptions shown here emphasize different skills. The waiter's first line is about "relationship building," an elegant way of describing customer service. A secondary aspect of the job involves organization. A server/waiter keeps track of different people and tasks, so good organization is essential. The final line on opening and closing duties shows responsibility and reliability. This example is from a student who normally only worked summers. The section at top-right shows how you might format dates to imply repeated summers. Employers expect students to have off in summer, so this does not set up any of the red flags otherwise associated with short-term employment.

Communication Jobs

Most Sociology students have interests in writing and hone their skills in a variety of formats and assignments. But since students in other majors also claim writing and communication as part of their skill sets, it is not an automatic advantage. If you are really interested in a job heavy on writing, you want to demonstrate practical experience. Internships or jobs that deal with content creation "show" claims to that skill, beyond that of a college degree. An example of such a position is shown below.

> **Editor** | Awakenings Art | Sunnydale, IL January 2019–June 2019
> - Provided feedback on content, corrected grammar, and designed general format of online magazine
> - Created opportunities for survivors of sexual violence to heal through artistic expression
> - Raised awareness of cultural taboos regarding sexual assault through content

This editor description includes critical thinking skills regarding content and communication in written languages. It also implies a skill for sensitively providing constructive criticism and feedback as well as a strong ethical orientation through the support of victimized communities. While not exactly evidence of intercultural fluency, the description highlights an apparent openness to deal with and discuss important and difficult issues. While the position is not technically creative, it promotes creativity in others. Employers place high value on such leadership. When I reviewed the description, I also recommended that the student include the software she used to design the magazine, but she did not feel sufficiently strong in that aspect to add it.

> **Social Media Coordinator** |Global Brigades-DePaul Chicago, IL 2018–2020
> - Managed Instagram and Facebook social media accounts
> - Promoted organization's brigades and fundraisers
> - Increased participation in brigades by 50% more students in my first year
> - Taught health self-care classes in Honduras and Ghana (in person)
> - Conducted vision tests and filled out pharmacy prescriptions

Communication technologies are one of the few areas in which young people are automatically assumed to be experts. However, you still must provide evidence of your skill; include the specific platforms used and the target audience if possible. The position shown above can be included either as Work Experience or as Extracurricular Activities in the resume. Even when the activities were part of a volunteer program, the organization depended on the student for their social media presence. The trips associated with membership show both a strong ethical orientation and intercultural fluency.

Education Jobs

Just by virtue of being in school, Sociology majors have expertise in education. However, that is not necessary to point out unless there are additional elements that display that expertise. In terms of both Work Experience and Extracurriculars, students tend to engage in educational environments in a variety of roles. Since all organizations need to train people, these experiences provide unique skills and expertise.

> **Teaching Assistant**| Inside-Out Prison Exchange Program | DePaul Univ. October 2019–March 2020
> - Designed and executed lesson plans on Restorative Justice
> - Led groups activities and managed classroom behavior of DePaul and incarcerated students
> - Provided individual education and emotional support

The skill for this job is obviously curriculum design and delivery. The language emphasizes critical thinking (design). Stereotypes about the audience, incarcerated individuals, often assume the applicant has a special capacity for dealing with difficult people and environments. This student also wanted to emphasize the importance of motivating learners, a form of leadership. The student was interested in serving incarcerated and formerly incarcerated individuals. The job description supported his intercultural fluency given that he had never personally experienced incarceration.

ESL Tutor| DePaul Community Service Organization | Sunnydale, IL January 2021–Present

- Designed instructional activities according to student needs
- Adapted student feedback to improve learning effectiveness
- Moderated and encouraged conversations to develop speaking fluency

While technically an educational position, this job description emphasizes interpersonal communications. It also demonstrates intercultural fluency or a desire to develop it. The job implies a strong ethical orientation through its serving of foreign-born populations who are stereotyped as vulnerable. Of course, this position is also relevant work experience for a job teaching English as a Second Language. Below you can find examples for Mentor, Orientation Leader, and Camp Leader.

Mentor | The Cities Project | Sunnydale, IL August 2016–March 2017

- Tutored mentee on positive coping approaches to overcome personal and educational issues
- Built a strong relationship through emphatic listening
- Evaluated effectiveness of program activities and worked with peer mentor to improve them

Orientation Leader | New Student and Family Engagement | DePaul Univ. March 2019–Present

- Oversaw administrative support for orientation programs for new college students
- Mentored first-year students on academic preparation, diversity training, and community building
- Facilitated group conversations regarding the transition to college life
- Resolved interpersonal conflicts among participants and employees

> **Camp Counselor** | Lifetime Fitness | Sunnydale, IL August 2016–March 2017
> - Designed, planned, and coordinated age-appropriate activities, including arts and crafts, skill-building exercises, and outdoor sports
> - Promoted skill development for beginning and intermediate swimmers
> - Escorted children on field trips and monitored behavior to ensure safety

Camp counselor is another summer-only job that can demonstrate a wide variety of skills. The role implies leadership and a certain extent of teamwork. The description provided above is more leadership-oriented since the camp counselor has authority over kids. The job also implies critical thinking and organizational skills in designing and executing activities. The job of "coach" can be described in similar ways.

Research and Critical Thinking Jobs

Because Sociology teaches students how to think about your experiences in the world, emphasizing critical thinking in the resume is necessary. However, I do not recommend using the term "critical thinking" in the Skills section. It is overly general and not well-defined. People even can mistake critical thinking for "criticizing" or having a negative attitude toward a particular system or object. While criticism can be the outcome of critical thinking, it is the process, not the outcome, that defines it. Instead, use the words recommended for methodology in Table 7.2 of the previous chapter. For the Work Experience and Extracurricular sections of the resume, critical thinking is shown by deconstructing the task performed into individual steps in a process and naming them precisely. As the most complete list of tasks associated with critical thinking, I recommend Bloom's Taxonomy of Learning Goals shown in Table 8.1. Instructors in K-12 through college level use Bloom's Taxonomy (Anderson & Krathwohl, 2005) to create learning objectives that are concrete, as well as student- and action-based. It offers a list of mostly verbs associated with various levels and types of analytical/critical thinking tasks.

All jobs provide workers with opportunities to apply critical thinking and to use the sociological point of view. Your description needs to identify the system in question and how it can be transformed or adapted (avoid using the word fixed) to

Table 8.1 Revised Bloom's Taxonomy of Action Words

Remember	Understand	Apply	Analyze	Evaluate	Create
Copy	Ask	Act	Advertise	Appraise	Adapt
Define	Associate	Administer	Analyze	Argue	Anticipate
Describe	Cite	Apply	Appraise	Assess	Arrange
Discover	Classify	Articulate	Break down	Choose	Assemble
Duplicate	Compare	Calculate	Calculate	Compare	Choose
Enumerate	Contrast	Change	Categorize	Conclude	Collaborate
Examine	Convert	Chart	Classify	Consider	Collect
Identify	Demonstrate	Choose	Compare	Convince	Combine
Label	Describe	Collect	Conclude	Criticize	Compile
List	Differentiate	Complete	Connect	Critique	Compose
Listen	Discover	Compute	Contrast	Debate	Construct
Locate	Discuss	Construct	Correlate	Decide	Create
Match	Distinguish	Demonstrate	Criticize	Defend	Design
Memorize	Estimate	Determine	Deduce	Discriminate	Develop
Name	Explain	Develop	Devise	Distinguish	Devise
Observe	Express	Discover	Diagram	Editorialize	Express
Omit	Extend	Dramatize	Differentiate	Estimate	Facilitate
Quote	Generalize	Employ	Discriminate	Evaluate	Formulate
Read	Give examples	Establish	Dissect	Find errors	Generalize
Recall	Group	Examine	Distinguish	Grade	Hypothesize
Recite	Identify	Experiment	Divide	Judge	Imagine
Recognize	Illustrate	Explain	Estimate	Justify	Infer
Record	Indicate	Illustrate	Evaluate	Measure	Integrate
Repeat	Infer	Interpret	Experiment	Order	Intervene
Reproduce	Interpret	Interview	Explain	Persuade	Invent
Retell	Judge	Judge	Focus	Predict	Justify
Select	Observe	List	Illustrate	Rank	Make
State	Order	Manipulate	Infer	Rate	Manage
Tabulate	Paraphrase	Modify	Order	Recommend	Modify
Tell	Predict	Operate	Organize	Reframe	Negotiate
Visualize	Relate	Paint	Outline	Score	Organize
	Report	Practice	Plan	Select	Originate
	Represent	Predict	Point out	Summarize	Plan
	Research	Prepare	Prioritize	Support	Prepare
	Restate	Produce	Question	Test	Produce
	Review	Record	Select	Weigh	Propose
	Rewrite	Relate	Separate		Rearrange
	Select	Report	Subdivide		Reorganize
	Show	Schedule	Survey		Report
	Summarize	Show	Test		Revise
	Trace	Sketch			Rewrite
	Transform	Solve			Role-play
	Translate	Stimulate			Schematize

(continued)

Research and Critical Thinking Jobs

Table 8.1 (continued)

Remember	Understand	Apply	Analyze	Evaluate	Create
		Teach			Simulate
		Transfer			Solve
		Use			Speculate
		Write			Structure
					Substitute
					Support
					Test
					Validate
					Write

improve it. You should also identify whether this transformation is for the benefit of customers/clients or for the organization. Finally, you can also describe how you transformed your own behavior to adapt to the system. Below you will find two examples emphasizing critical thinking skills.

Merchandising Intern| Paper Source | Normal, IL September 2019–December 2019

- Analyzed brand messaging and offerings from competitors
- Adapted product descriptions for use on Salesforce
- Evaluated various elements of the Paper Source brand experience
- Crafted a customer profile based on the target demographic

Research Assistant | Evaluation of Dodd-Frank's Impact on Community Banks | Spring 2019

- Synthesized quantitative assessments of Dodd-Frank legislation on community bank performance and profitability
- Compared the impact of Dodd-Frank on financial institutions of varying organizational sizes and structures
- Profiled adjacent policy developments and drafted future policy proposal

Organizing Work Experience and Extracurricular Sections

I hope you find these job descriptions useful as you create your resume. Copying descriptions that particularly fit your experience, sensibilities, and goals is a good and painless way to start building your own resume. Once you have made an exhaustive list of all activities and experiences available to you, you can decide what and where to include each component.

Ideally, you already have in mind a job or types of jobs that interest you. Carefully examine the job description and select which specific elements of your resume you want to emphasize. Organize all your entries in chronological order from most recent to oldest. That includes Education, Work Experience, and Extracurriculars. Any deviation in the chronology is considered a red flag. However, you can subtly manipulate the order of your entries to display the skills most relevant to a particular job. Among your options, you can:

Omit certain activities. This strategy is needed if you have too many elements in your resume to fit on one page.

Move certain items from Extracurricular Experience to Work Experience or vice versa. Exercise caution when moving things to Work Experience. Anything in that section should be substantial in terms of both quality and amount of time; the Extracurriculars section is much more flexible. It can include a variety of experiences if they are relevant to either the job description or demonstrate your potential as a worker. Remember, you can also include experiential learning experiences here that you acquired in school if you describe them in the same format as your jobs or internships.

Revise the names of the sections. You can name the Extracurricular section anything you want and can list almost any experience you can imagine. You might call it Volunteer Experience or Other Experience. If the content is outside the traditional resume, make sure the experience you describe is relevant to the job. Under limited circumstances you may even consider changing the title of the Work Experience section. For example, some students create a single Experience section that combines diverse types of activities if they have too few elements to create separate sections. It might also work if you lack work experience.

As a final reminder, the arrangement of the sections and their relative emphasis also matter. If you have job-relevant work experience, that should be the most visible section on your resume. If you don't, I recommend starting with the Education section. That will immediately direct employers to your major and tell them if you are seeking a position as a student worker or an intern. If you are looking for your first full-time job, the Education section will show them your graduation date and when you will be available to work.

Conclusion

Application materials should be designed using the language of employers, which comes from the language of business and management. Two relevant characteristics of business language are action and positive biases. For the Work Experience and Extracurricular sections, it is recommended that you start your description sentences with verbs. Choose verbs that convey the right connotations for the skills mentioned in the job description and other organizational materials. Be as specific as possible, avoiding empty or overly general verbs. Remember that work experiences in unrelated jobs in retail, hospitality, communications, and education offer evidence of NACE transferable skills. All jobs can be described as providing valuable skills, in particular critical thinking and decision-making. Finally, you can organize the order and names of these different sections of your resume to best fit the job you are applying for.

Discussion Questions

1. Recall any incident where you used the language of Sociology and other people did not understand you. Share it with your classmates.
2. Do these incidents of differences in language have anything in common (audience, situation, context)?
3. Does the use of action language make people more likely to act?
4. What are the social consequences of emphasizing verbs in language?
5. Thinking of your own use of language, does it tend to be positive, neutral, or negative?
6. What are the social consequences of positive language?
7. What do you mean personally when referring to "critical thinking?" What do you think employers think when they hear that term?

Action/Reflection Activity

1. List all Work Experience and Extracurricular positions and activities you have had since age 16. For this first list, try to be as thorough and expansive as you can.
2. Review the lists of Socioemotional, Transferable, and Technical skills from the previous chapter (Tables 7.4 and 7.5). Assign one to three skills to each activity from those lists. Then go online and find a list of verbs associated with both the activity and the skill. For jobs with critical thinking skills, use Table 8.1.
3. Write three to five sentences describing each activity in your list. Use high-quality verbs. You can copy any of the examples in this chapter if they apply.
4. Exchange your activities and descriptions with your classmates. Try to improve them following the principles outlined in Chaps. 6, 7, and 8.
5. Review and note the positions and activities that provide your best profile for a potential job. If you have a particular job or type of job in mind, make sure to prioritize the most relevant elements.
6. Organize the information into sections that maximize the visibility of your most pertinent skills, positions, and activities. You can exchange items among the Education, Work Experience, and Extracurricular sections and change section titles to reflect your best profile for the job in question.
7. Review your Education, Work Experience, and Extracurriculars lists. Decide which skills you want to emphasize in the Skills section of the resume. Create your list of skills.
8. Exchange your complete resume with classmates. What might you improve as a result?
9. Ask a third party to review your resume (Career Center advisor, instructor, family member, or friend).

Works Cited

Meyer, J. W., & Rowan, B. (1977). Institutionalized organizations: Formal structure as myth and ceremony. *American Journal of Sociology, 83*(2), 340–363.

Anderson, L. W., & Krathwohl, D. R. (2005). A taxonomy for learning, teaching, and assessing: A revision of Bloom's taxonomy of educational objectives. *Educational Horizons, 83*(3), 154–159.

An Identity-Based Job Search 9

The most basic elements of career management are strategies designed to find and apply for jobs. Transformations in capitalism make it unlikely that you will spend your entire career in a single job, organization, or industry. You will have to continue applying for jobs if you want to improve or "move up" in your career. At certain levels of an organization, you will need to apply for internal positions and possibly compete with outsiders to get a promotion. Furthermore, you may find yourself stagnating in your current job and want to move to another to get a raise or a promotion. Take internal applications as seriously as you would take those submitted to a new organization. You may also have to apply for outside jobs even if you would prefer to stay with your company. Sometimes just having an alternative offer is enough to motivate your boss to fight for you.

If you are using this book, your goal is to get your first job after graduation or an internship to gain experience. If you have seriously followed the content and activities so far, you are already strong in two components of employability: professional identity and skills. You know who you are and who you want to be as an individual, a sociologist, and a community member or leader. You should also have some idea of what you can offer an organization and how to express that potential in a language employers understand. Even with this knowledge, it is normal to still feel like you are not ready for a full-time job or even a part-time internship. Reaching for your goals can create anxiety. It may help you to know that I have never had to tell a Sociology student that they are not qualified for whatever position they wanted. On the contrary, I spend a lot of effort just trying to convince students that they are ready; they just need to take the risk. In the interest of thoroughness, let us review a general version of what you already know about yourself.

You are a highly ethical person, professionally invested in making the world better. You are part of a scientific discipline, trained in both quantitative and qualitative methods to answer diverse questions and respond to decision-making situations. You have strong transferable skills in at least intercultural fluency and communications. With expertise in discrimination and oppression, you can help organizations avoid or minimize them. You have additional expertise in particular industries and groups. Your extracurricular activities and jobs have developed alternative skills and expertise that complement your sociological self. YOU ARE READY!

This chapter will guide you, step by step, through the job application process. Now it is time to stop thinking and reflecting about who you are and what skills you have. It is time to identify jobs and organizations that interest you. I divide the job application process into the following four steps. The rest of the chapter will concentrate on strategies and challenges for implementing them.

STEP 1: Summarize Your Interest, Skills, and Needs
STEP 2: Perform a Job Search
STEP 3: Create a Cover Letter(s)
STEP 4: APPLY, APPLY, APPLY

STEP 1: Summarize Your Interests, Skills, and Needs

The identity work provided in Part I of this book was designed to help you find, refine, and express a professional identity. You have discovered what makes Sociology unique and what values the discipline implicitly promotes. You have integrated those elements into your own personal interests, values, and action orientation. Part II is focused on how to uncover your skills. Depending on your personal life and educational experiences (e.g., freshman versus junior), you should be able to discover what positions would fit you. Summarize your interests, skills, and expertise into one document. This summary will be a useful source of keywords for your job search.

My recommended tool in drafting this summary is the asset map shown in Fig. 9.1. Using it can help you approach the labor market with a broader and more holistic view of your potential. The tool was developed by Pfeifer and Stoddard (2019) as part of their pedagogical strategy for experiential learning. They devised it to help freshmen (in their case Engineering students) realize what they had to offer a community-based project. Their assumption was that if students recognized their own skills, they would feel empowered to actively participate in the project. The same principle applies to the job search: reviewing what you have to offer will

STEP 1: Summarize Your Interests, Skills, and Needs

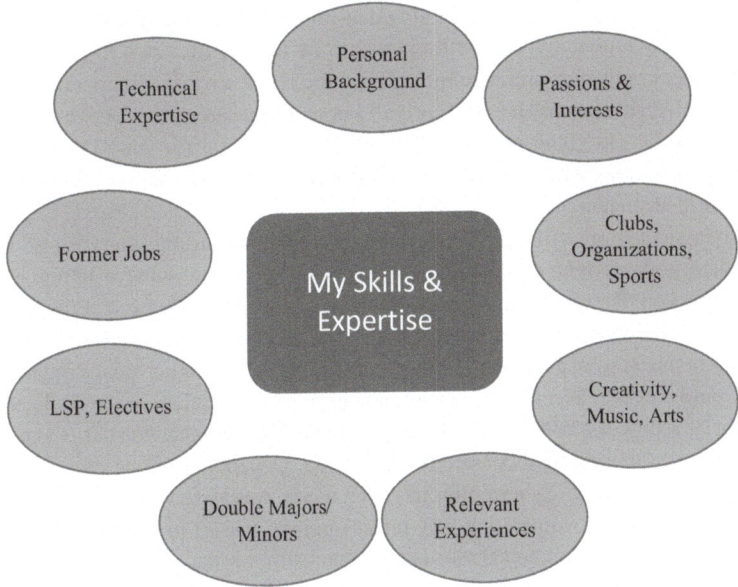

Fig. 9.1 Global Asset Map

make you more likely to apply for jobs. The tool is flexible enough to accommodate students at all levels of their educational career.

In this step you also must define, at least broadly, what you are looking for in a job or internship. Geographic location will limit your options. Many recent graduates, for example, prefer to stay near their college or family. Decide if you need to narrow your search to a particular metropolitan area or prefer to target a region or state. Maybe you want to avoid the big expensive cities but undertake a national search. Another option is to move to another country. These choices depend on your personal circumstances, but remember that narrow searches are likely to produce fewer opportunities.

Another issue you need to decide about is work modality. The technology for remote work has existed for decades, but it was only with the disruptions of the COVID-19 pandemic that remote work became a widely available alternative. Remote internships are an interesting option, but they limit your learning about the organizational culture and your interaction with co-workers. Fully remote full-time positions remain a minority in the labor market. *The Washington Post* reported that 15% of job postings on LinkedIn in October 2022 were for remote positions, while

50% of total job applications were aimed at remote jobs (Bhattarai, 2022). Many companies have gone hybrid, with options to be in the office two to four days a week. Other companies prefer people to be in the office, even if on paper they offer remote or hybrid options. It is too early to know if there are career penalties (salaries, promotion) to going remote or hybrid. It is important for you to decide first what is acceptable. Then carefully investigate the company's position on remote and hybrid arrangements.

Having a clear idea of your needs and expectations regarding salary is also key. Calculate your current or potential expenses so you know what a living wage means for you. Research the average payment of a position to see if it fits within your needs. Remember to adjust for the cost of living in your location. You may have to revise your aspirations or your living expenses. Create a salary range that you would consider acceptable. Do not, however, mention salary in the application or interview process. You do not want to give the impression that you care too much about it, even though that's perfectly reasonable. Depending on the organization, salaries are negotiable after an offer has been made. And if you are a part of a marginalized group or a woman that may mean forcing yourself to negotiate your salary; reluctance to negotiate salaries is a known cause of income disparities across certain groups (Dreher & Cox Jr., 2000; Mazei et al., 2015).

When it comes to salary, internships are a special case. My position as a sociologist is that all internships should be paid but that is not the reality of the world we live in. Some unpaid internships offer opportunities for networking, preferential access to full-time jobs, and transformative learning experiences. While I hope that if you are ever in charge of internships you will make a point of paying students as part of your sociological ethics, do what you must at the beginning of your career. If your personal circumstances rule out an unpaid internship, look for alternatives. For example, some universities offer internal grants that will provide you with funds while doing an unpaid internship.

Benefits tend to be non-negotiable but equally important to salary. Think about the importance of health insurance (including dental and vision), paid vacation days, profit-sharing and stock options, tuition reimbursement or loan repayment, and retirement benefits compared with wage levels. Do you prefer to be paid more or to have your organization contribute the money to your retirement? If medical insurance is of special concern, make sure to check its quality (cost, co-payment, deductible, network) before accepting a job offer.

STEP 2: Perform a Job Search

Time now to find an open position for a job or an internship! There are several ways to find jobs. Two alternatives are an exploratory or a keyword search. The exploratory search is best if you are still unsure of what kind of jobs are out there. Its purpose is to offer you an idea of the labor market. The keyword search is more direct and focused on finding a specific type of position. It works best when you have a sense of what you are looking for. Specific instructions for doing both types of searches follow.

Exploratory Search

The exploratory search is less about finding an internship or a job (although it may happen) and more about getting to know the landscape of the market. The economy in the twenty-first century is truly diverse and complex. New products, services, industries, and jobs are constantly born. Old positions get renamed. An exploratory search can open your mind to the possibilities. I hope that now and throughout your career you will continuously explore your options by keeping up with important developments in your selected field. To begin, do general research about organizations and the positions they post. Industry lists are a useful tool of exploration. You may find lists such as Best Companies to Work For, Best Non-profits to Work For, and Most Socially Responsible helpful. Some of the most prominent national and international lists are sketched out below.

Newsweek National publication. Issues an annual list of the 500 most socially responsible companies in the United States. Produces and displays scores on environmental, social, and corporate governance dimensions. May not apply to your geographic location.

Fortune National publication. Lists 100 Best Companies to Work For. May not apply to your geographic location. Skewed toward big corporations in services, technology, and retail. Worth investigating with an open mind. Big companies offer better salaries and benefits. Some have Community Relations Departments or Foundation arms that may be good options for sociologists.

The NonProfitTimes Nonprofit management publication. Offers a national list of best nonprofits organized by employee size. Created by Best Companies Group, a consultant to organizations on employee engagement.

Glassdoor Job service website. Collects and shares employees' opinions of workplaces along with other useful information. Includes lists for private and nonprofit organizations. Lists are customizable by location and industry.

Monster.com Job service website. Publishes a list of the best nonprofits at the national level and direct links to current jobs posted by those companies. Allows you to sign up for notifications when a job with your specifications becomes available.

Zippia Job service website. List of best jobs in the private, nonprofit, and public sectors. Lists can be filtered by states, large metropolitan areas, and industries.

Refinitiv Consulting and development company specializing in financial technology and data, including sustainable financial solutions. Provides list of the 100 most socially responsible companies in the world. Their methodology includes workforce relationships, human rights, community relations, and product responsibility. Skews toward big corporations.

Ethisphere Consulting firm dedicated to creating, measuring, and promoting ethical standards among companies. Global list of highly ethical private firms customizable by country and industry. Skews toward big corporations.

In addition to these lists, local publications and organizations create lists of the best companies within a particular geographic area. Do a Google search for these local lists and explore a few of them. From both national and local lists, select a few companies you find interesting, go to their Careers or Jobs pages and see what is listed. Think deeply about what you could do for them and how they fit your interests. Decide which organizations, if any, you want to follow on a regular basis. Create a list of keywords with positions, activities, and any other requirements you think warrant exploring further. You can eventually use the keywords for a more focused job search.

The exploratory search is particularly useful when looking for ideas for what to do, but it can be helpful even if you are sure of your path. Some Sociology students are certain that they want to become lawyers or social workers, and even know what area of law or social work they want to practice. Doing an exploratory search can help determine your "fall back" options. Having a second option is not a reflection of your potential or your commitment to your career. Life happens and people change with it. I wanted to be an international correspondent and travel the world. Once I got to practice a little journalism, I realized I did not have the disposition to move from one small story to another. I prefer longer forms of writing with enough time to do deep analysis. Once I learned this about myself, I switched from journalism to academic Sociology.

Keyword Search

A search using a job service is like a bibliographic search for academic papers. You start with a concept or topic and perform a keyword search. The resulting asset map will provide you with starting keywords. Although unlikely to produce any job postings under the keyword Sociology, there are jobs out there that ask for degrees in social science. If your initial search generates no good results, try another keyword. If your search provides good jobs, continue using that keyword in the future. Each good hit will yield additional, and hopefully more precise, keywords. If you have trouble getting started, Table 9.1 lists potential keywords that my students have found useful. This is not a complete list, and it may not be appropriate for your interests, but it provides a starting point.

For internships, the best sources of listings are the Career Center and student employment office at your university. You can find a myriad of jobs that can lead you to different career paths. Universities have departments similar to other types of organizations, and you can find positions that develop and use a variety of skills. Also consult the job service website Handshake. This service is aimed at students and recent graduates, and it connects universities to employers. It offers the best selection of internships and entry-level jobs.

I want to take a moment to emphasize the importance of internships for all students. Students who already know they want to be social workers, lawyers, or another occupation tend to believe they do not need an internship. Keep in mind that you cannot practice an occupation like law or social work until you finish the required advanced degree and are licensed in the field. Having internships along the way will provide you with information and skills to use in the future. Interning or working part-time for a local firm can give you a sense of the day-to-day operations of the profession.

I have also encountered students so enamored with one organization and their mission that they cannot imagine working anywhere else. If this describes you, contact the organization directly and request an opportunity for an internship or to

Table 9.1 Potential Keywords for Job Searches

Potential Keywords	
Positions	Topics
Fundraising Professional	Foundation
Event Planning	Training
Event Coordinator	Education
Program Support Specialist	Youth/Child Development
Grant Writer	Sustainability
Programming Coordinator	Community Relations
Volunteer Coordinator	Program Evaluation
Community Program Planner	Diversity
Philanthropy Program Manager	Public Relations
Program Associate	Healthcare
Program Assistant	Immigrants/Refugees
Development Manager	Social Media
Communications Manager	Communication
Media Coordinator	Harm Reduction
Engagement Manager	Vulnerable Populations
Service Advisor	Mental Health
Giving Coordinator	Evaluation
Program Manager	Data Analytics
Development Officer	Admissions (University)
Research Assistant	Legal Aid
Research Associate	Policy
Analyst	Learning Experience Design
Care Coordinator	Instructional Design

volunteer. Monitor the organization's recruiting webpage continuously to catch the right opportunity. However, your desire for a job or internship may not correspond with the organization's current needs or your skills. Instead of waiting for an opening, think about what kind of job could enhance your skills and expertise to prepare you to eventually apply to your dream organization. You can find a job in another organization within your desired area or with the characteristics you admire. Maybe they provide the same type of service or product, serve a similar population, or share the values you respect. Use this information to perform a keyword search. Gaining entry to certain very competitive industries such as museums, film, or music can take a while. For some, earning a position by doing extensive volunteer work is an unstated but real condition for landing a paid job.

Another special situation is when you cannot decide between two or more career paths. Everything sounds equally appealing (or unappealing). This is not an uncommon position to be in at any stage in your education. You have two options: either collect more information or choose an experiential position in the field.

Attend a few events like career fair panels or do a couple informational interviews. However, if you have done your due diligence, talked to people in the field(s), and are still undecided, your best bet is to go for an experiential activity like an internship. It is better to experiment in the lower pressure environment of an internship than in a formal job. As noted above, for internship searches, I recommend using Handshake. While this job service website also includes full-time jobs, it caters directly to university students and recent graduates. Many employers, Career Centers, and other university departments post their internships on the site, and it is free for students. Don't procrastinate. Choose one organization or position to start; flip a coin if that helps.

STEP 3: Create a Cover Letter(s)

The cover letter is an artifact predating the Internet and, from a certain point of view, can be considered obsolete. It is also redundant, since it repeats the information contained in your resume. Many employers continue to request it, while others skip it altogether. There is a great chance that you have never written a letter, let alone a commercial one. My students usually express an incredible amount of anxiety over this activity; they want me to teach them how to do a cover letter. Trust me when I say that after all the work of reflection and resume creation you have done, the cover letter is easy. Commercial communications are standardized. The writing is no mysterious art.

The cover letter is an instrument of persuasion. By contrast, the resume is an informational tool which depends on the reader to make the connections between its content and the position being sought. The purpose of the letter is to convince the recruitment and selection reviewer that you are the right fit for the job. You persuade by making a direct connection between your experiences and the job description. The cover letter allows you to select the most relevant information in your resume and tell the reviewer exactly how it relates to the position. If you have a qualification or a pertinent reason not included in your resume, then you need to customize your resume a bit more before you submit your application.

The rules of business language apply to the cover letter. Concentrate on the positive and avoid bringing attention to the negative. Your job is to present and frame your experiences in the best possible light. It is the interviewer's job to find or detect your potential shortcomings. For example, as a student you may lack direct experience for the position. Your letter should emphasize the transferability of other experiences and never mention any deficiency.

Cover Letter Components

1. **Date:** Located at the top of the letter, it can go either on the left or the right. I prefer the right-hand position, to provide contrast to the rest of the content. Use the date of your application, not the date you wrote the letter. If you are submitting online, you need to create a separate file for each job application. Keeping all your cover letters will provide you with a record of your application history, which may be useful when you apply more than once to the same organization.
2. **Employer Information:** Place the employer's address and contact information in the top left corner (see Fig. 9.1). From an information perspective this makes little sense since the employer already knows this. However, including this extra detail indicates that you are not just randomly applying to as many jobs as possible without carefully analyzing your suitability. To omit it or even enter inaccurate information may signal a lack of interest and/or conscientiousness. Of course, always insert accurate information. Check the spelling of the organization's name and how it is written on the website or other documents. Don't overlook the use of grammatical marks, capitalization, or possible idiosyncrasies in how it is written. Omitting the information altogether is the biggest mistake. If possible, include the name and title of an individual and address the letter directly to them. This information is sometimes included in the job posting as a contact person for questions. Indeed.com has a guide on where to find that information if it is not listed there. Alternatively, you can address your letter to the Human Resources Department or the Hiring Committee. Again, do a little online research to make sure you use the official name the company uses.
3. **Form of Address:** Always start the actual contents of your letter with the salutation, Dear, followed by the person's or the department's name. Avoid gendered and marital status assumptions such as Dear Sir, Dear Madame, or Dear Ms. The exception to this rule is when the person states a preferred form of address. Modern norms of address consider it acceptable to use the name alone (i.e., Dear Jack Black).
4. **Introductory Sentence**: Writing the first sentence of your letter can produce anxiety. Do not waste your time trying to be original in your opening sentence; using stock phrases is perfectly acceptable as part of business communication. The only reason to spend time on this component of the letter is if you are applying for a writing or communications job. In that case, crafting a unique and beautiful sentence that demonstrates your skill in the area is necessary. I recommend mentioning the exact position name you are applying for since a hiring

STEP 3: Create a Cover Letter(s)   145

manager may be dealing with more than one position at a time. Some good introductory sentences are:

My name is Martha Martinez, and I would like to apply for your position xxx....
I was excited to see that Company ABC is hiring an xxx....
I was excited to learn of this job opportunity for xxx from my xxx....

5. **Qualifications Evidence:** Here you need to show at least three reasons why you would be a good hire. Order these reasons by fit, first mentioning your experiences and qualifications that directly apply to the position. Begin with your accomplishments, technical skills, and expertise in the area. Transferable skills and socioemotional skills should be included later or not at all.
6. **Concluding Sentences**: This is where you thank the hiring manager for their time and attention, reiterate your interest in the position, and state where and how you can be contacted (usually by email and telephone number).
7. **Signature:** Introduce your signature with the word "Sincerely," followed by a comma. Allow some blank spaces, add your formal signature, and then print your name and contact information below the signature. Create an electronic form of your signature so you can easily add it to each letter.

Cover Letter Example

Figure 9.2 provides a skeleton of the elements of a cover letter to use as a guide. There is no "right" or even "best" cover letter. Each one must be adapted to the job posting and your qualifications and interest. Even when considering those factors, there are several combinations of experiences and attributes you may want to emphasize. Figure 9.3 provides a listing for a position in community outreach in a nonprofit health organization copied directly from Indeed.com. In my experience, both the position and the organization would attract some Sociology students and be appropriate for a recent graduate. As you can see, the description is extensive, a little repetitive, and includes what we would consider transferable and socioemotional skills. I have marked in yellow the distinct elements that I would consider important to include in my cover letter.

Figure 9.4 provides an example of what I would consider a solid cover letter for the job posting. I am not personally looking for a position, but I tried to make the letter reflect the experiences and interests of my students. I decided to underline the formal name of the position as stated in the job posting to make it easier to identify in case the organization is hiring for different jobs at the same time. Each element included pertains to something in the job posting. First, the posting emphasizes mission and values, without mentioning them specifically. Therefore, I went to the

---

Date
Title and Name
Organization
Address

Dear xxx:

I am writing to apply for the position of xxx... posted on xxx. As requested, I am attaching xxx.... I am interested in the position/organization because xxx... My studies as a sociology major (modify to reflect required level of study) have helped me develop xxx (customize to fit the job)

Expertise/Skill 1

Expertise/Skill 2

Expertise/Skill 3

I believe my experience in xxx... can be an asset to your organization.

You can reach me at xxx (e-mail address) or 555-555-5555. I hope I will have a chance to discuss the position with you in the future. Thank you for your time and consideration.

Sincerely,

Signature

Name
Address
Phone Number
Email Address

Fig. 9.2 Cover Letter Template

company's website and identified those elements. From there I extracted the exact words posted to describe my interest (health equity) to align my personal interests with the mission of the organization. I also selected three organizational values to mention as my own (taken from a list of eight): respect, inclusion, and efficiency. I considered those three to best reflect my own identity. In the first paragraph I also mentioned my BA and the fact that I have a driver's license which were both requirements of the position. In the next three paragraphs I offered evidence of my suitability for the job. First, I used retail experience as a proof of interpersonal communication skills. I also provided a philosophy associated with that skill (active listening) and related my secondary skills. The second paragraph integrated written communication with Spanish translating skills. The final paragraph focused on my expertise with the target population.

STEP 3: Create a Cover Letter(s)

Position: Community Engagement and Outreach Coordinator

Healthcare Alternative Systems, Inc. (H.A.S.) is a 501 (c) 3 non-profit organization providing behavioral health services to Chicago and the surrounding communities. We offer a continuum of programs addressing substance abuse, mental health, adolescent issues, family relationships, and more. Every year, H.A.S. serves over six thousand individuals.

Essential Functions:

Community Engagement and Outreach Coordinator organizes initiatives designed to promote the organization's programs and its services to the community. Develops relationships with community leaders and serves as the organization's liaison with various constituents.

Community Engagement and Outreach Coordinator Responsibilities:

- Supports the organization's mission, vision, and values; adheres to its policies and procedures in carrying out the responsibilities of this position.
- Develops and maintains partnerships with other organizations in the community to increase awareness and support.
- Serves as liaison between the organization and the community to deliver successful programs.
- Represents the organization in the community through numerous engagement activities.
- Maintains full knowledge of programs and services provided.
- Administers organizational programs aimed at addressing the needs of the community.
- Performs specials projects and related duties as required or as assigned by supervisor.

Skills:

- Interpersonal Skills: Ability to interact effectively with diverse individuals and build effective working relationships.
- Administrative Skills: Good organizational and time and management skills. Effectively completes assignments and meets deadlines.
- Communication Skills: Strong written and verbal communication skills, good public speaking skills, confident communicator with demonstrated ability to present information effectively to groups and individuals.

Community Engagement and Outreach Coordinator Qualifications:

- Must be able to maintain a valid driver's license and automobile license.
- Must have own vehicle.
- Flexible, dynamic and engaging with strong interpersonal skills.
- Strong communicator with skills in writing and public speaking.
- Ability to always represent the organization professionally.
- A team player with the ability to forge new partnerships that bridge people and organizations.
- Able to prioritize under deadline pressure.
- Excellent with time and task management skills, able to work independently.
- Familiar with the latest public relations trends and best practices.
- Bilingual in English/Spanish is preferred.
- Possession of valid Illinois driver's license and willingness to use personal vehicle in course of employment.
- H.A.S. requires all staff to work onsite.

Education and Experience Requirements:

- Bachelor's Degree in related filed.
- Previous experience working in related discipline preferred.

Fig. 9.3 Job Posting Example

May 10, 2023

Hiring Committee
Healthcare Alternative Systems, Inc.

Dear Hiring Committee:

I am writing to apply for the position of <u>Community Engagement and Outlook Coordinator</u> posted on Indeed.com. As requested, my resume and a copy of my driver's license are attached.

As someone who hopes to dedicate my life to the improvement of health equity, I believe that the approach of H.A.S., which emphasizes inclusion and respect, but also efficiency of treatment, is an enormous step in the right direction. My sociological training with a specialization in health inequality has shown me the pivotal role community leaders play in promoting local health services and relieving suffering effectively.

My two years working in retail customer service have enhanced my interpersonal skills and made me realize the importance of active listening in building relationships. Only by first listening can we figure out how to help people. My customer service experience also has given me insight into how to negotiate and deescalate situations.

I have extensive experience with several forms of communication, including posting on social media and writing opinion articles and reports. I am fully bilingual and have done both written and simultaneous translations at a professional level. This could be beneficial in creating relationships and promoting your services among the Spanish-speaking community.

I am a first-generation college graduate and an immigrant, which I think offers me an awareness of the significance of culturally sensitive and equal access to mental health treatment. I suffered from a debilitating mental health condition during my student years. While I was fortunate to have medical insurance, my own limited resources helped me understand the vital relationship between health and economic issues. That inspires my commitment to maintaining affordable residential programs like those your organization provides.

I believe that my focus on health inequality, my communication skills, and my capacity to empathize with those who are suffering could be assets to your organization. I hope to have the opportunity to discuss the position with you in the future. You can reach me by e-mailing mmarti75@depaul.edu or calling 555-555-5555. Thank you for your time and consideration.

Sincerely,

Martha Martinez-Firestone
990 W. Fullerton Ave.
Chicago, IL 60622
555-555-5555
mmarti75@depaul.edu

Fig. 9.4 Cover Letter Example

At this point, I decided that a longer letter would be counterproductive. Listing too many elements decreases the impact of each one individually. For this letter, I emphasized communication, the skill that is listed most often in the job posting. I also decided to use my personal background to reinforce my fit for the position and the organization. The job posting lists other key skills that I did not include. I could have made a different letter focused on my administrative skills, my attention to detail, my public relations knowledge, and my experience in public speaking. Any of those letters could make a compelling case. It is impossible from the job posting to predict exactly what kind of letter would be the strongest. That is the kind of information that a direct contact in the organization might be able to provide you. Missing that, I would recommend that do your best and do not sweat or overthink it.

STEP 4: APPLY, APPLY, APPLY

Your goals are your own, but I strongly believe that all Sociology students should follow a formal process of career exploration and development. Be intentional in building your future. Researching positions and organizations is a vital part of this process. However, no research in the world will be effective if you do not apply for jobs. Be confident and bold in your application process. Your goal should be to apply for as many positions in as many organizations as possible that fit your interests. Do not self-censor; the responsibility of deciding if you are qualified belongs to the employer. Tell your community and your network that you are actively looking for a job. Currently, LinkedIn is the main social media platform for career networking. Take the information from your resume and use it to create a LinkedIn profile. Mark yourself as looking for work. If your family and friends use Facebook, let them know you are looking for a job and ask for their help. Spread the word in other online lists or groups as appropriate.

I usually recommend that students set a goal to submit at least one application a day. If you have followed the recommendations in this book, the rest is a numbers game. There is a random component to the process. You do not control what happens on the employer's side. Do not get discouraged if your first applications go unanswered. Keep applying. However, remember to ask for help from the people around you. Talking to a Career Center professional about your search can help you find ways to adjust your strategy.

Conclusion

An identity-based job search is comprised of four steps. Step 1 summarized the work you did in Part I to create a professional identity and the recontextualization of your skills and expertise described in Part II. This step also includes determining your personal requirements from a position, such as geographic location, work mode, salary range, and benefits. Step 2 concentrated on finding specific internships or jobs either by an exploratory or keyword searches. Step 3 detailed how to create a customized cover letter and modify your resume to fit a particular position and organization. Step 4 offered motivation to just start applying for specific jobs and circulate your intentions among your personal community and professional network.

Discussion Questions

1. What are your current job-related needs?
2. Would an exploratory or keyword search be more relevant to your situation?
3. Do you feel prepared to apply for a job?
4. What additional experiences do you think you need to land your dream job?
5. What part of the job search process gives you the most anxiety?

Action/Reflection Activity

1. Create a complete asset map. List at least three items in each category.
2. Perform an exploratory job search.
   (a) Select one local and one national list of organizations.
   (b) Select three organizations per list.
   (c) Look for job postings on the organization's website.
   (d) Determine at least one job that you could do in an organization.
3. Perform a keyword job search.
   (a) Using your asset map or the words in Table 9.1, do a keyword search in a job service.
   (b) Select at least three jobs that interest you.
   (c) Determine additional keywords for a future search.

4. Create a cover letter.
   (a) Select one job from either your exploratory or keyword search. Depending on your needs, you may select an internship on Handshake instead.
   (b) Create a customized cover letter for the position.
   (c) Customize your resume for the position.
5. Apply for a job or internship.

Works Cited

Bhattarai, A. (2022). The great mismatch: Remote jobs are in demand, but positions are drying up. *The Washington Post*. Retrieved from https://www.washingtonpost.com/business/2022/11/27/remote-jobs-economy/

Dreher, G. F., & Cox, T. H., Jr. (2000). Labor market mobility and cash compensation: The moderating effects of race and gender. *Academy of Management Journal, 43*(5), 890–900.

Mazei, J., Hüffmeier, J., Freund, P. A., Stuhlmacher, A. F., Bilke, L., & Hertel, G. (2015). A meta-analysis on gender differences in negotiation outcomes and their moderators. *Psychological Bulletin, 141*(1), 85.

Pfeiffer, G., & Stoddard, E. (2019). Equitable and effective student teams: Creating and managing team dynamics for equitable learning outcomes. In K. Wobbe & E. A. Stobbard (Eds.), *Project-based learning in the first year: Beyond all expectations*. Stylus Publishers.

Part III
Career Management

A Sociological View of Managerial Behavior

10

Many Sociology students I have met over the years are not overly fond of studying managers or management. They think managers are not properly aware of or worried about social problems, and they do not see themselves as ever wanting to become one themselves. Managing is something other people do. You probably share this view. However, given the bureaucratic organization of work in the twenty-first century, advancing a career implies eventually becoming a manager. Substantial increases in salaries are almost always tied to supervising people. This is true for the for-profit sector, nonprofit organizations, and government positions. Many jobs also include managerial functions without offering the title or the pay associated with them. Even in temporary and part-time jobs, many experienced employees are asked to do managing functions, including planning and training, without getting paid or recognized for them. Most workers are under the direct supervision of a manager, and that person will have a disproportionate effect on your personal career. Even those who avoid a bureaucratic structure altogether by becoming self-employed will have to manage themselves and their own productivity. There is no escape.

As an economic sociologist with specializations in organizations and entrepreneurship, I find managers fascinating subjects. I have also taught Business undergrads and advised MBA students. In some ways, they are like you. They worry about unpaid internships, low minimum wages, and environmental degradation. They want meaningful and authentic relationships with co-workers, superiors, and subordinates. I have no scientific evidence, but my guess is that they tend to be more optimistic than social scientists about the potential of both technology and reason to help us solve social problems.

© The Author(s), under exclusive license to Springer
Nature Switzerland AG 2023
M. A. Martinez, *The Employable Sociologist*,
https://doi.org/10.1007/978-3-031-41323-0_10

Obviously, someone does not need an undergraduate or graduate degree in Business to become a manager. Managers come out of diverse undergraduate degree programs and have varied interests and dispositions. Someone majoring in Accounting is different from a Human Resources or Marketing major. Yet, regardless of differing dispositions and skills, there is something that can be identified as managerial culture, and Sociology has much to say about it and about the institutionalized practices that fall under the umbrella of Management Science.

Sociology faculty tend to have a critical, meaning negative, view of the managerial profession, particularly when someone is trying to manage us. The concept of managerialism described by Bellah et al. (2007) critiques managers as excessively focused on narrow objectives like profits instead of more broadly defined social goals. They also criticize them for a certain degree of "manipulation." The difference between persuasion and manipulation is rarely clear. In academic settings, we have the freedom to vocally criticize and ignore both Management Science and our managers. You will no longer have that freedom. The use of positive or neutral language is just one of the many explicit and implicit rules of the workplace. While I cannot provide you with an exhaustive list of rules of conduct to guide how you will have to behave, I can provide you with a general overview of the history and culture of management. The rest of this chapter will explore both issues.

Scientific Management as Culture

Understanding, rather than stereotyping and judging, managerial culture will be a key component of your career development work. As the sociological imagination tells us, historical context provides unique clues to why social systems are what they are. Management Science has its roots in the beginning of the twentieth century and has been strongly influenced by two other disciplines: Engineering and Psychology. Fayol and Taylor, the parents of Management Science and of the paradigm called scientific management, were both engineers. If you are interested in modern interpretations of their influence in contemporary management, read *Management and Ideology* by Judith Merkle (2022).

The problem facing managers during the Industrial Revolution, and which remains the guiding goal of Management Science, is how to take inputs and put them through a transformation process to become outputs. In the for-profit sector, outputs must always be worth significantly more than the cost of inputs. That includes the cost of the labor or work applied to the process of transformation. Profits are a measure of efficiency in the creation of wealth, and in theory a measure of social good. Most managers are surprised to learn that the end goal of some organizations is not profit but to provide a benefit to society. The relationship between inputs and outputs is normally referred to as productivity. Scientific management marks the point when control became the main preoccupation of managers and Management Science. Control is about making people follow particular procedures at the right moment. This general preoccupation becomes more specialized as organizational processes are separated into departments. The preoccupation with control extends to inputs, processes, people, environments, markets, and political forces.

The first theory in Management Science was rather redundantly called scientific management. This theory is the first of many "rational" theories and techniques designed to improve the relationship between the inputs and outputs of organizations. Just in Time Production, Total Quality Management, Kanban Methods, Management by Objectives, and the most current one, Agile Management, are only a few examples of rational management techniques. While originally conceived for production, these techniques have been applied to the service sector as well as to marketing, sales, human resources, and finance. One of the underlying principles of Management Science is that control is desirable, possible, and ever expanding and improving (Beniger, 2009).

The second problem of Management Science is derived from the first: how to motivate a group of people to work together in an organized fashion toward the goals of the organization. Part of the problem is about persuading individuals to commit to goals from which they benefit only marginally. The second issue is how to reduce conflict among employees, assuming conflict reduces efficiency. More current managerial theories aim to channel that conflict toward the achievement of organizational goals. Scientific management theory assumed that people would respond rationally to managers, and usually depended on supervision and incentives to increase their productivity. Early on, researchers found that this assumption about human behavior was incomplete and even wrong.

Managers discovered that people did not respond well to the excessive supervision created by scientific management. We now call this kind of supervision micromanagement. They also learned that monetary incentives were only partly successful in motivating workers. The failure of this sort of rational technique was often attributed to the "irrational" attitudes of workers.

Workers have always been more rational than professional managers acknowledge. The lack of success of incentives and control often stem from a lack of trust between employees and their supervisors. Not without cause, workers have historically assumed that the incentives were temporary, and that managers would eventually reduce their pay but maintain the higher levels of production. In fact, a key empirical fact of the history of Western capitalism during the twentieth century has been that gains in productivity benefit employers and investors a lot more than the workers themselves. The imbalance in the distribution of the wealth generated by greater productivity is particularly extreme in today's environment where the effects of neoliberalism and the last wave of globalization that started in the mid-1980s continue to be felt (Schwellnus, Pak, Pionnier, & Crivellaro, 2018). This imbalance is one of the main causes of the wage inequality we are experiencing now.

Distrust of management is not the only reason workers may resist greater productivity. "Efficient" work arrangements and technologies can have negative effects on the health, safety, and quality of workers' personal lives. Managers sometimes fail to recognize and care about these "externalities," a term economists coined to describe the negative effects of capitalism that do not directly affect profits. Workers are not being irrational when they worry about the side effects of work arrangements; they just have different priorities and a longer-range timeframe to consider than modern organizations usually do. Another reason for the apparent lack of "rational" behaviors is the variety and complexity of the social contexts that workers inhabit. Workers do not exist in isolation and their lives are not limited to work relations. They are part of broader social systems and institutions that also affect their decisions and behaviors. The problem of social coordination in the presence of multiple coexisting and overlapping social systems, each associated with its own cultural elements and dynamics, cannot be solved by the linear thinking of rational methods.

The Human Relations School

On a deeper level, it is highly debatable whether it is ethical or even possible to "control" human behavior in the pursuit of a narrow goal. To address this ethical concern, Management Science has borrowed directly from Psychology. Elton Mayo, father of the famous human relations school of thought, dedicated his life to creating a different paradigm to explain and affect workers' motivations. He was an Australian psychologist interested in testing scientific management's principles. Through a set of experiments he designed to evaluate the effects of lighting on worker productivity, he accidentally discovered that the amount of attention and recognition these experimental groups received increased their productivity regardless of their lighting conditions. This experiment led to his creation of the human relations school of thought and became the first of many techniques developed to increase employee commitment to the organization. The discovery put emotion and social dynamics at the center of managerial attention. From a sociological perspective, recognition of the workplace as a form of social organization that is influenced and connected to the general culture and other forms of social structures was a move in the right direction. His theory opened the door for Sociology's additions to the study of management. In particular, the human relations school and its descendants support Max Weber's insight (first published in 1905) that internalized forms of control, basically internalized culture, are a more powerful and less contested form of control that those based on external mechanisms (Barbalet, 2008). In the same way, social pressure exerted by personal networks is more effective and less ethically contested than the bureaucratic and technological mechanisms of control at the heart of Scientific Management. The insights of Mayo and his descendants do not necessarily see softer forms of control as a problem of ethics. At least at the ideological level, they view such policies as a solution that benefits everyone—both the organization and the workers.

Mayo's theory also addresses a separate problem of control faced by managers: the external environment. Because organizations rely on external sources for inputs, a concept known as resource dependence, they attempt to create structures and strategies to acquire resources. The history of organizations during the twentieth century is characterized by an increase in specialized departments and areas of knowledge designed to control a particular aspect of functions and environments. For example, the role of the Marketing Department is to control or at least influence markets by using tools that affect demand. Public Relations Departments are set up to maintain relationships and try to control media information about the organization. Each department within an organization generally develops a particular logic of action and a corresponding rhetoric. These different orientations can create conflicts between departments that may affect the success of their organizations (Kaufman, 2014). While in theory all departments should support the goals of the organization, each has its own orientation and can be blind to the needs and orientation of other departments. The role of Human Resources Departments goes beyond dealing with employer-employee relationships, including efforts to preempt damaging legislation or sanctions by the government (Kaufman, 2014). Given the evolution of twentieth-century capitalism and Western democracies, the government has become the most influential force affecting the survival of organizations. And one of government's main preoccupations has been to regulate employer-employee relationships, although not always in favor of workers.

Sociological Contributions to Management Science

Besides the work of Weber on incentives, what has been the role of Sociology vis-à-vis Management Science? Economic Sociology and Organizational Studies have produced theories used in Management Science. Weber's work on bureaucratic control has been incorporated into traditional Management Science (Clegg & Dunkerley, 1980). Similarly, sociological theories such as systems theory (Luhmann, 1984), social capital (Burt, 1982; Bourdieu, 1986), network/actor theory (Latour & Woolgar, 1979; Grint & Nixon, 1991; Bloomfield & Best, 1992), contingency theory (Woodward, 1962), population ecology (Hannan & Freeman, 1977; Carroll, 1985), and global commodity chains (Gereffi, 1996), among others, have been adapted for managerial purposes. The key word is "adapted." Sociological theories were never designed to help solve problems of efficiency and coordination within organizations, but rather to understand how they actually work and their role in society. Unlike Management Science, Sociology does not assume that the goals of an organization are worthwhile. Nor does it accept the assumption that maximum efficiency, however it is measured, will create the greatest amount of social good. Management Science takes sociological knowledge—our models, concepts, and categorizations—strips them of critical components, and directs them toward the accomplishment of the organizational goal. Economics does something similar with Marxism. It takes critical analyses of capitalism, reduces them to their application for efficiency, and "naturalizes" them by treating market forces like gravity: neutral and inevitable.

The critical approach of Sociology provides its students and graduates with advantages over their Business major counterparts. Sociologists have not internalized the goal of making organizations well-functioning machines and students have had practice in learning to question the value of implicit and explicit goals. Students of Sociology know that organizations should, but not always do, serve society. Even when they do, they tend to cater to or most benefit a few of their most powerful members. Sociologists believe that sometimes efficiency should be sacrificed to accommodate other types of positive social outcomes. This form of critical thinking is a powerful transformative force, one that also helps clarify how organizational goals relate to your own.

As a Sociology graduate transitioning from school to your first job in your career, the rational and human relations ideologies will have equal impact. Because culture and scientific knowledge are cumulative, both the rational and sociocultural logics coexist at the same time in the organizational landscape. While in theory the rational and the emotional/social are not necessarily opposed to each other, in the day-to-day of business they often become diametrically opposing ways to approach the decision-making process. Good management theoretically balances both the rational and the emotional/social. Good management, however, can be very scarce.

In the real world, rampant exploitation often substitutes for good management. It takes a certain amount of skill and dedication to remain consistently committed to either rational or emotional/social strategies and values. Finding the right balance in which the rational and the emotional/social reinforce each other requires the work of both a genius and a saint. Sometimes ideologies of reason are dominant in certain departments (such as Technology, Production, Accounting, or Finance) while sociocultural narratives have more influence in others (consider Human Resources, Community Relations, or Social Responsibility). Despite departmental differences, workers permanently face ambiguity and conflicts between these two orientations.

Human Resources Departments

The department with the most overarching impact on management-employee relations across the organization is Human Resources (HR). This department is tasked with the problem of finding and organizing people and their work in a way that will facilitate the accomplishment of organizational goals. The key to understanding its point of view is as a tool for managing relations with government. It specializes in interpreting and applying local-, state-, and federal-level labor laws. Human Resources Departments originated in the 1920s, just as the American government started to develop a more active role in regulating labor relations. Prior to that, it was believed that any government intervention into the labor market, even to prohibit child labor, violated the Constitutional right of both employers and employees to enter into whatever contract they considered acceptable (Kaufman, 2014).

Since then, government regulation of employment relations has increased, although enforcement expands and contracts according to political winds. HR is responsible for navigating these changing environments and making sure that the organization fulfills all legal requirements of employment, including anti-discrimination efforts. The goal of HR is not necessarily to improve the lives of workers or end discrimination, but to protect the organization from government sanctions. It also must protect the organization against exposure to legal actions by its employees. Those working in HR may want to protect and improve the lives of employees, but the function of the department is to protect the organization. Just consider the emphasis on confidentiality when dealing with sexual harassment cases, salary differences, or medical leaves. While there may be legitimate concerns about protecting individuals from retaliation and social pressures, the lack of transparency often protects the organization more than the individual.

Traditionally, HR Departments have adopted a very legalistic and risk-averse orientation focused on minimizing the risk of incurring penalties from government or lawsuits from individuals. Its attention to issues like confidentiality, privacy, professionalization, protection against unjust termination, and anti-discrimination stems from a concern both with moral and ethical standards and with government intervention. Just like Legal Departments (also called Offices of Special Counsel or Organizational Counsel), they are charged with protecting organizational interests. Sometimes the interests of the organization overlap with those of the workers; other times they conflict. What is legal is not always ethical or vice versa. Whenever approaching the study of HR Departments, sociologists must be aware of these potential conflicts between goals and cautious about disclosing information.

Traditionally, Human Resources Departments have also handled the recruitment and selection of personnel for all positions. This function is defined as a problem of control. The goal is to find the best method for attracting and hiring the candidates who best fit the organization and its positions. The hiring process presents an interesting control problem since performance in a particular position cannot be known until an employee has done the job for a certain length of time. Organizations need to identify a hiring process that will help them predict a certain level of quality in a candidate's future performance. One such process is the use of initial temporary contracts lasting from three to six months. At the end of that period, the organization and its managers decide whether to make the position permanent through an open-ended contract. This practice tends to be more common in entry-level and low-paying positions. For new hires with a history of work experience and promotions, the risk of a proper fit is presumed to be lower. As noted in the skills section of this book, all parts of the application and hiring process are designed to maximize a fit within both the position and the organization. The next chapter will discuss the selection process further. For now, we will just mention that from a sociological perspective, no system can be completely rational; it is always being measured in relation to and interacting with culture. Any tool developed is likely to be affected by gender, race, ethnicity, and the class dynamics of the current society.

Avoiding Capitalism and Managers

Undergraduate students commonly develop negative attitudes toward Management Science through their study of Sociology. As a Sociology faculty myself, I find criticizing managers and economists a favorite part of my job. Management Science, including scientific management, the human relations school, and its successors, were created within the context of industrial and market capitalism and the demands of profitability. Sociology implicitly and explicitly criticizes the narrowness of this approach and its goals. Yet, sometimes we confuse the need for change or reform with an impulse for destruction. Capitalism has both positive and negative consequences in its uneven distribution of goods and privileges across society. While revolutionary ideologies may dream of supplanting it with a new system, few would exchange it for Soviet-style socialism or a return to the pre-industrial Middle Ages. Even Marx, for example, singled out aspects of modern capitalism to preserve. He considered the industrial division of labor necessary but wanted its profits to be reinvested into enriching society. Similarly, Weber, with all his critiques of bureaucracies, still considered it one of the most important innovations in human history. Capitalism and Management Science are simultaneously the best and the worst things that have happened to humanity.

In searching and applying for jobs, undergraduate Sociology students may tend to steer away from career choices linked to capitalism and managerialism. This can be a losing strategy. Systems created after the Enlightenment, what we call modern, including management and capitalism, are unavoidable. If you assume that capitalism and managerialism are only negative and certain types of organizations are better, you may be not only shortchanging your career but setting yourself up for exploitation or alienation. Some of these assumptions worth reevaluating are examined below.

Nonprofits Are Better

Many Sociology students look for jobs in the nonprofit sector thinking that a lack of profits means higher ethical concerns. And while there are many worthy nonprofits out there, to assume that an organization is ethical just because it is nonprofit is dangerous. Likewise, to presume that a for-profit cannot be good or ethical is the most pernicious and self-limiting assumption Sociology undergraduate students may make. As an organizational scholar, I can tell you that the purposes and working conditions within both for-profits and nonprofits vary widely. On average, because nonprofits depend on their reputations to attract donors, they may indeed be more aligned with the values of their donors, but those values may not be the same as yours. For example, the National Rifle Association (NRA) is a nonprofit, however I would not consider it a positive force in American society.

Despite not being focused on profits, nonprofit organizations are affected by capitalistic pressures. Their main preoccupation is to fulfill their missions, which can vary as much as their assumed needs of society and the visions of their founders. They can include such disparate goals as creating art, ending homelessness, lobbying for prison abolition, preserving the environment, or even promoting hunting and gun rights. Missions cannot be accomplished without resources. Those resources are produced by capitalist activity which may include a history of exploitation, even if it occurred in the past. Think, for example, about the origins of the money given out by the Gates Foundation. Nonprofits get their resources from four sources: the government, foundations, wealthy individuals, or small donors. Resource dependency theory (Pfeffer & Salancik, 2003) tells us that there is a general need for organizations to adapt to the demands of those who control key resources. In their search for funding, many nonprofits end up compromising their mission and values. Those that try to depend solely on small donations may risk insolvency.

When it comes to employee-employer relations, nonprofits may be willing to sacrifice their workers in service of their mission. They tend to pay significantly lower wages as well. Low wages are partly a function of having fewer resources in general, but they also are related to how the nonprofit sector defines efficiency. To continue functioning, they must provide donors with evidence of their efficiency, however that is defined. Unfortunately, the most common measure is the lowest ratio of overhead compared to money disbursed to the mission. The result is the lowest possible wages for the workers who make the mission possible. That's why even when nonprofits have ample resources, they do not tend to use them to increase the salaries of their own employees. Therefore, they are exploiting them.

The reverse assumption is the belief that for-profit companies must be bad for society. Since "good" depends on how you define social value, this question is not open to empirical investigation. The efficient use of resources for production is a benefit for society, but overproduction and overconsumption have negative social consequences. We need food, even some processed foods, along with jackets, houses, shoes, laundry detergent, etc. Some people in the world still have difficulty accessing basic necessities, let alone small luxuries. There are for-profit companies committed to bettering the world; profits enable them to expand their operations. Until a system to replace capitalism comes along, it would be short-sighted for you to dismiss companies that are trying to improve basic living conditions and provide sustainable jobs.

Smaller Is Better

Big corporations exert both negative and positive effects on society. They are very visible, and they tend to hold the attention of the media and the public. CEOs of some large companies may have as much impact as the heads of countries, even exercising policies over people they do not represent. From an employer-employee perspective, large organizations tend to be more advantageous. They often provide better pay, more stable jobs, and can afford to develop their employees. Big corporations are also likely to have Human Resources Departments. While we have noted some of their shortcomings, HR Departments can also make workers' lives easier, particularly more predictable. With the enactment and enforcement of labor laws in the United States dependent on politics at various levels of government, labor conditions, including benefits and pay, vary. In the absence of clear government rules, HR policies constitute a first line of defense for workers. In the absence of HR, workers are subject to the knowledge and goodwill (or their lack) of individual managers for fair treatment. When problems arise, there may be no potential avenue for recourse.

Some big corporations are bad employers, but not all. Disney may have a reputation for ruthless corporatism when defending its intellectual property, for example, but it is considered a good employer. On the other side of the spectrum, Amazon is infamous for its unreasonable treatment of high-level workers (such as firing people when they cannot work because of illness) and its extreme exploitation of its warehouse employees. While you probably would not want to work at Amazon, you should also know that many small businesses provide similarly bad working conditions and low pay. But because they are small, their bad work environments do not draw the attention of the media, society, and government, or incite calls for accountability. They may not be as efficient at extracting productivity from workers, but that does not make them better employers.

Minority-Owned Is Better

Support for minority-owned business should be considered part of our sociological ethics. However, that ideal should be tempered by the reality that minority-owned companies may not be better employers than other types of organizations. Minorities bring their own cultures and subcultures to their organizations. Sometimes this means greater understanding and concern about the issues their employees face, other times it merely replicates the structures of inequality and exploitation seen elsewhere. Consider this example. El Milagro is a tortilla and chips factory founded by Mexican immigrants in Chicago in the 1950s. Its products are among the most authentic and highest quality available in the United States. Yet, more than half a century later, it is still relying on underpaid immigrant labor and has been cited for labor law violations. During the pandemic, it created a mandatory, seven-day work week. Sociological studies tell us that immigrant businesses play a central role in the exploitation of their co-nationals (Cranford, 2005; Rosales, 2014). Certainly, there are many admirable minority-owned businesses, but do not assume that just because they are not white-owned, they will provide better working conditions.

Beyond the problems you can create for yourself by overidealizing nonprofit, small, and minority-owned organizations, hopes of escaping capitalism and managerial culture are futile. For-profit, large corporations have a dominant position in society and many other types of organizations follow their model. Practices, technologies, and tools normally originate in the for-profit sector and are replicated by nonprofits. Some people think that this encroachment of for-profit methods, particularly the standards of efficiency used to measure the inputs in nonprofit and government organizations, has intensified since the 1980s through the political ideology of neoliberalism. Sociologists working in the for-profit and public sectors must always be mindful of the pressures of managerial techniques filtering into nonprofits. These may not be the most suitable techniques for government and nonprofit organizations to achieve their more complex and ambiguous goals. For sociologists, this conflict presents an opportunity to contribute practical insights to the world by examining whether those measures and processes follow or drive the logic of the missions of organizations.

Conclusion

By law, tradition, and material incentives, managers are obligated to prioritize the goals of their organization and its survival above the well-being of the individuals within it. Coexisting rational and socioemotional motivations at play in management discourse and strategies may conflict with each other. Managerial orientation can reflect a variety of factors, including the department within the organization or the manager's educational background (including college major). Managers are professional framers who use stories based on different logics of action depending on the issue or context. Sociology students and graduates trying to evade the effects of capitalism and managerialism by joining nonprofit, small, or minority-owned businesses should recognize that these choices carry their own disadvantages. We live in a capitalist society. It is impossible to not be affected by its workings. Management Science and managers are under pressure to follow a capitalist logic of efficiency regardless of the sector. Sociologists can uniquely help organizations by uncovering conflicts between missions and measures.

Discussion Questions

1. How would you describe your relationship with capitalism?
2. What is your opinion on the advantages and disadvantages of managerialism?
3. What philosophy of management do you prefer (scientific management/human relations)?
4. Is it possible to find a balance between rational versus socioemotional ways of management? Why or why not?
5. Do you prefer to work for a nonprofit, small, or minority-owned organization? Why or why not?
6. Can for-profit companies be good for society? Why or why not?
7. Do nonprofits need to be efficient in their mission?
8. Are you willing to sacrifice your personal well-being for another purpose? Why or why not?
9. Do you think exploiting others is justified if you are (or have been) exploited yourself?

Action/Reflection Activity

1. Locate and contact a manager in an industry or organization within your community. Request an interview either in person or online and ask the following questions:
   (a) How did you become a manager?
   (b) Have you formally studied Management Science? Is it needed to be a manager?
   (c) What is particular or different about your personal management style?
   (d) Do you see contradictions within the values or practices of your organization? How do you deal with them?
   (e) What are the biggest challenges of being a manager in your type of organization or industry?
   (f) What are the rewards of being a manager?
   (g) What are the most crucial factors in a good worker-manager relationship?
   (h) What do you wish your subordinates would do differently or know?
   (i) What would you recommend to a recent graduate entering your organization/industry?
2. Write a three-four-page Reflection Paper about the role of managers.
   (a) What are the most important components of the role?
   (b) What new things have you learned about it?
   (c) What misconceptions did you have about it?
   (d) Do you see yourself becoming a manager?

Works Cited

Barbalet, J. M. (2008). *Weber, passion and profits: 'The Protestant ethic and the spirit of capitalism' in context.* Cambridge University Press.

Bellah, R. N., et al. (2007). *Habits of the heart, with a new preface: Individualism and commitment in American life.* University of California Press.

Beniger, J. (2009). *The control revolution: Technological and economic origins of the information society.* Harvard University Press.

Bloomfield, B. P., & Best, A. (1992). Management consultants: Systems development, power and the translation of problems. *The Sociological Review, 40*(3), 533–560.

Bourdieu, P. (1986). "The forms of capital." *Cultural theory: An anthology (2011)* 1: 81-93.

Burt, R. (1982). *Toward a structural theory of action.* Academic Press.

Carroll, G. R. (1985). Concentration and specialization: Dynamics of niche width in populations of organizations. *American Journal of Sociology, 90*(6), 1262–1283.

Clegg, S., & Dunkerley, D. (1980). *Organisation and Society.* London: Routledge.

Cranford, C. J. (2005). Networks of exploitation: Immigrant labor and the restructuring of the Los Angeles janitorial industry. *Social Problems, 52*(3), 379–397.

Gereffi, G. (1996). Global commodity chains: New forms of coordination and control among nations and firms in international industries. *Competition & Change, 1*(4), 427–439.

Grint, K., & Nixon, D. (1991). *The sociology of work.* Polity.

Hannan, M. T., & Freeman, J. (1977). The population ecology of organizations. *American Journal of Sociology, 82*(5), 929–964.

Kaufman, B. E. (2014). The historical development of American HRM broadly viewed. *Human Resource Management Review, 24*(3), 196–218.

Latour, B., & Woolgar, S. (1979). *The social construction of scientific facts.* Sage.

Luhmann, N. (1984). *Soziale Systeme: Grundriß einer allgemeinen Theorie.* .. Frankfurt am Main.

Merkle, J. A. (2022). *Management and ideology: The legacy of the international scientific management movement.* University of California Press.

Pfeffer, J., & Salancik, G. R. (2003). *The external control of organizations: A resource dependence perspective.* Stanford University Press.

Rosales, R. (2014). Stagnant immigrant social networks and cycles of exploitation. *Ethnic and Racial Studies, 37*(14), 2564–2579.

Schwellnus, C., et al. (2018). "Labour share developments over the past two decades."

Woodward, J. (1962). *Industrial organization: Theory and practice.* OxfordUniversity Press.

The Selection Process   11

Once you have submitted your application, you enter the selection process. Technically, this includes the initial review of your resume by a Human Resources or other professional handling applications. In this chapter, I will take you through what happens after an application successfully passes the initial review. Although the employer controls the selection process, you will discover that it is based on standardized and ritualized procedures developed by managerial sciences. Employers see their selection process as a time-tested and rational approach for finding the best candidate for a position. Their dual objective is to find the best "fit" for their organizational culture. From a sociological perspective, this process is a series of rituals and ceremonies (Meyer & Rowan, 1977) based on myths of reason and science. Participation in these rituals assesses a candidate's capacity to successfully join a particular culture. Successful applicants will expertly fulfill the expected role. With careful preparation and foresight, applicants can increase their chances of success.

This chapter will help you prepare for that process. It starts with a description of the general dynamics of a typical selection process and includes both expected elements and potential variations. The kinds of tests you may encounter follow. The bulk of the chapter covers selection interviews, the most intense and manipulable element of the selection process. You will find a guide for interview preparation and a list of potential questions. I will also introduce the STAR (Situation, Task, Action, Result) system for answering interview questions and will provide examples of responses that Sociology students have developed. Each answer emphasizes different transferable skills.

The two main techniques used in the selection process are standardized tests and structured behavioral interviews. The process begins with a screening interview,

© The Author(s), under exclusive license to Springer Nature Switzerland AG 2023
M. A. Martinez, *The Employable Sociologist*,
https://doi.org/10.1007/978-3-031-41323-0_11

usually by phone. This initial short contact will double-check your availability and confirm some resume qualifications. If successful, you will be invited to take part in a more involved selection process. For any given position, you will face a series of scaffolded tests and interviews. Their goal is to try to predict your future success in both the intended position and long-term membership in the organization.

Generally, Human Resources professionals manage the initial stages of the selection process, and the later stages are handled by the hiring departments. The order of activities may vary, but typically concludes with an in-person meeting with your potential boss and co-workers. Final interviews may be one-on-one or a group interview in which three to six people may ask you questions. In light of the recent COVID-19 pandemic and based on the nature of the company, the final step may be online rather than in person. This is increasingly more likely today with work teams and operations dispersed among different physical locations and more positions based completely online. An online job may entail only online interviews, but not necessarily.

The process can range anywhere from two weeks to several months. It will be shorter and more informal in nonprofits which have fewer resources to dedicate to the selection process. Larger organizations tend toward longer and more complex selection processes. They can be haphazard and interrupted at any time. Always, whatever step you are in, ask about what steps to expect next and the approximate timeline. Expect every step to be potentially delayed by the organization. Asking for a deadline gives you a reason to follow up and show your continuing interest. Even when organizations say they are in a hurry to hire, the process always takes longer than expected. It is not because people are lying. For you, your job search is the highest priority; for HR and hiring personnel, it may be just one of many activities on their calendar. Or plans might change in the blink of an eye. One or two bad profit quarters or new leadership may lead to a sudden hiring freeze or downsizing. Organizational-level restructuring may erase some positions and create new ones. You need to be patient and not take either rejection or delays personally.

Selection Tests

The association between selection tests and jobs has a long history. Before the formal foundation of Psychology and Management Science, literacy, industry or job knowledge, and physical skills were used to measure employability. In China, the Imperial Examination has been used to fill civil service positions since the Tang Dynasty from 618–907. Modern, scientific selection methods have been systematically designed, used, and studied for about 100 years (for a review of the history of selection tests, see Vinchur & Bryan, 2012). Rooted in Psychology, the tests assume that there are significant individual differences, those differences can be measured, and those measures can predict future job success. It is ironic, however, that the first "scientific" tests used anthropometric measurements based on the proportions of the human body to predict moral character and job performance. While anthropometric measures are still used as predictors of health (i.e., body mass index) and safety measures for physical work (think of the equivalent of height requirements for amusement park rides), they have been completely discredited as general predictors of job performance.

Current hiring practices include the use of a battery of cognitive, personality, and skills tests. Cognitive tests attempt to measure an applicant's ability to learn; employers assume that good cognitive abilities will mean faster and higher quality learning of job activities. Depending on the company and the job, those skills may include arithmetic, reading comprehension, spatial relations, and emotional intelligence, or other variations. Few positions that Sociology undergraduates are likely to seek will entail physical or knowledge tests. Exceptions are jobs requiring more "technical" knowledge such as research methods (both quantitative and qualitative) or language skills. While not exactly a "test," applicants may also be asked to make a presentation on a job or industry-related topic. The presentation is designed to allow you to demonstrate your communication skills and expertise on a specific topic.

Chapter 6 described the role of personality in relation to job choices, particularly the association between conscientiousness and job performance. The popularity of personality tests in hiring practices ebbs and flows. HR professionals may think that certain personalities are more employable or better suited to a particular job or their organization. The five-dimension personality model is the most popular test in this category, but not the only one used. A personality test sometimes used in the selection process was developed by cardiologists. They created a profile of Type A personalities: people who tended to be competitive, ambitious, very organized, impatient, and highly focused on work goals. People labeled as a Type A personality were predicted most likely to have a heart attack (Riska, 2000). Later, they designated other personalities by additional letters (B, C, and D) and ascribed certain character and behavior traits to each type.

According to the five-dimensions model, Type A personalities are positively correlated with extroversion and neuroticism and negatively correlated with agreeableness (Morrison, 1997). I have seen certain companies favor Type A personalities. Amazon, for example, has been very vocal in its preference for such individuals, whose highly competitive and less agreeable personalities match the culture developed by company founder Jeff Bezos. Other organizations avoid Type A individuals like the plague. It is impossible to be certain what personality profile a company seeks in general or for a particular position. You can get some clues about the degree of assertiveness versus agreeableness they desire by examining the language they use on their websites to describe their employees. You may also find clues in the language of job ads.

Sociologists tend to be skeptical of cognitive and personality selection tests as indices of job capacity. Studies show only moderate correlation between cognitive ability, training, learning, and job performance. Studies vary between 0.30 and 0.70 correlation between cognitive skills, training, and learning, and between 0.40 and 0.50 for cognitive ability and job performance (Ones, Viswesvaran, et al., 2005). Correlation, of course, is not causation. Even at their best, tests only explained around 54% of variation in job performance. The evidence linking personality to job performance is more ambiguous, but stronger when matching a particular dimension of personality with a specific job (Whetzel, McDaniel, et al., 2010). Sociology believes that "personality" (labeled by classic sociologists as social character) has a strong social and cultural component. While there may be some inherent biological elements to personalities, they are developed through socialization in specific cultural environments (Parsons, 1958). Sociologists see personality as the internalization of social patterns developed during our formative years. Because we live those years in capitalist economies, our personalities are the product of class and class relations. Your answers in a personality test are less about your inherent traits and more an externalized expression of your habitus and historical generative categories of perception, appreciation, and action (Pickel, 2005; Meisenhelder, 2006). Not surprisingly, certain personalities traits, particularly extroversion, are more common within certain geographic areas, cultures, and nations. Using personality as a predictor of job success may lead toward discrimination. The good news is that conscientiousness tends to be widely distributed across groups, and is, therefore, not linked to race, ethnicity, or nationality (Heine, Buchtel, et al., 2008).

Regardless of the limits and unintended consequences of tests as predictors of job performance, employers rely strongly on them. A "failed" test may mean the difference between getting a job offer or being eliminated from the pool. You should take tests seriously. Be aware of their nature and create the right conditions for taking them if they are online. You might even want to look for sample tests on the Internet for practice. But I do not recommend extensive studying or even trying to "game" personality tests. There is too much ambiguity and variation in what employers are seeking to be worth the effort.

Selection Interviews

While some organizations may skip tests, you are unlikely to get a job without interviewing. Preparing for interviews is a crucial factor for your job search success. Anxiety usually reduces effective interview performance. Strong preparation can be a strategy for managing anxiety. Hopefully, you will have done a fair amount of research on the organization and the position before you applied. If not, be sure to do that before your first interviews. Knowledge of the organization and the position show conscientiousness and therefore employability. You should compile the following information before you start interviewing at an organization:

- Names of any family, friend, acquaintance, or fellow alumni in the organization (they may help you find the rest of the information)
- Organizational mission, vision, values, target market or "client," and products/services provided
- General knowledge of the industry, including main competitors or peer organizations, networking or industry organizations, and famous figures
- Recent media articles on the organization or industry (the past 2–5 years) to quickly review
- Main transferable, technical, and socioemotional skills associated with the position
- Average and range of salaries for the position, preferably considering your location
- Key requirements/benefits/characteristics you would like to have in the job

Before discussing the content of interviews, we should understand their nature as a social interaction. During the last few decades, interactions between people have become less structured, deferential, and formal but rather more egalitarian. Interviews are exceptions to this trend. They are still highly scripted rituals akin to a dance. You need to follow certain steps, but you also must pay attention to your partner so you can respond to their movements. In this case, the interviewer is the lead partner. You will be expected to present yourself in a more careful and "conservative" manner than in other social interactions. That includes cues about dress norms. The expected attire for interviews is generally business formal for both men and women. For men, this is always a suit and dress shoes. Although women have more flexibility in what to wear, they are also subject to more "judgments" or assumptions about wardrobe. You may remember the controversy of a few years ago about women not being allowed on the floor of the US House and Senate wearing sleeveless shirts or dresses. Some environments are still very conservative. For women, I recommend pant or skirt suits and two-to-three-inch heels. In addition to the general dress code, companies may have their own particularities. I know that for Harley Davidson, the motorcycle company, showing up to your interview in a suit is the kiss of death.

You should also be conservative in your language. Imagine that you are talking to an authority figure, to impressive people like the pope or Barack Obama. You want to be precise, smart, and formal. Never, ever, ever, swear in an interview. Unless you are applying for a job in the training or education fields, avoid saying you "educate" people. I have heard Sociology undergraduates use that word in the context of improving race relations and gender categories and pronouns. While I expect that as a sociologist you will in fact educate your organization on a variety of social issues, a Gen Xer like me can feel disrespected or challenged to hear it coming from a Millennial or a Gen Zer.

Also be aware of the physical distance between you and the interviewer. You don't want to create anxiety by invading someone's personal space. Six feet apart is considered the gold standard. Carry a mask in case you need it. There are people that are still uncomfortable with non-masked interactions. If you are wearing a mask, be sure to explain why you need it. To keep your mask on while the other person does not may be interpreted as neuroticism. You are entitled to safety, but you need to be aware of social judgments and defer to your host. Be especially alert to verbal and non-verbal cues. For example, physical contact (such as shaking hands) should follow the lead of the interviewer.

You may consider all these little rules an imposition or a form of domination. You are right. Because you want a job, the employer has power over you. The good news is that the interview is only a couple of hours of your life. Think of it as demonstrating that you can practice self-regulation to fit an audience, even if you will not be expected to exhibit similar behaviors on the job. Eventually, as you progress through your career, you will be able to be more yourself, and possibly even change the job application standards for new hires in your organization.

Basic Interview Questions

Remember that the interview questions are intended to determine your qualifications and your fit in the organizations. Therefore, they tend to follow clear templates. The wording and framing may vary slightly, but the questions will focus on two fundamental areas: (1) Why do you want to join this organization or job and (2) Why should we hire you? Expect some of the following basic questions:

Basic Interview Questions

- Why do you want to work here?
- What do you know about this company/organization?
- What are you looking for in a new position?
- Why did you decide to apply for this position?
- Where do you see yourself in five years?

These simple, open-ended questions offer you an opportunity to demonstrate your knowledge and passion. Your answers should always be sincere, concrete, and positive. In doing your background research, find something good about the industry, organization, or position to justify your interest. Here are some options for what you might say:

- You like a specific aspect of the mission, vision, or values.
- You personally use the product or service.
- The organization or industry may be related to your own personal identity (gender, race, age).
- The organization or job helps create community or positive relationships with the community.
- The job or organization would allow you to learn or deepen a certain expertise or skill.
- The employer is recognized for its good personnel policies.
- The employer is a leader in their industry.
- You have a contact or friend who works at their organization and recommended it as a good place to work.

The question about where you see yourself in five years is designed to see whether your plans are compatible with the nature of the position. Hiring someone new is expensive. Employers hope you will stay for a few years. Put another way, they hope that they, not you, get to decide when your employment is over. Anything that indicates "longish" commitment is a satisfactory answer. You might mention other positions that appeal to you within the organization. Just like any other aspect of the job search, there may be situations in which the conventional wisdom does not apply. For example, if you aspire to become a lawyer, you may first want a job as an administrative assistant or paralegal in a law firm. Since you will eventually have to leave to go to school, saying you plan to stay in the position for two years would be sufficient. From a sociological perspective, it would be better for you to see the employer-employee relationship as a limited economic exchange; seeing it as a personal or emotional relationship is an example of false consciousness. But influenced by the human relations school, employers want your loyalty and enthusiasm. Saying you only want a job for the money is the only wrong answer to this type of question.

Another central element of the interview will be behavioral questions. They may be situational, asking what you would do in a particular situation, or patterned behavioral, asking you to provide an example of past behavior in a certain situation. The specific questions will vary considerably depending on the organization and the position. I recommend searching online for sample questions related to the position and preparing some answers in advance. Frequent lines of questioning of this sort include those shown below.

Situational Behavioral Questions

- How quickly do you adapt to technological change?
- What do you think our company/organization could do better?
- How do you feel about working weekends or late hours?
- How would you manage personal conflict with a co-worker?

Patterned Behavioral Questions

- What do you consider your three greatest strengths? Can you provide an example of X?
- Give an example of how you have managed a challenge in the workplace before.
- Give an example of when you showed leadership qualities.
- What type of supervisor helps bring out your best performance?

Answering Behavioral Questions with STAR

Just like every other aspect of the application process, answering behavioral questions is highly ritualistic. Core answers are the same whether they are framed as situational or patterned behavior. Ideally, your answer will address the question while simultaneously conveying your best skills. The most-used and expected format for answering all behavioral questions is through stories that follow the STAR method in which you describe a Situation, Task, Action, and Result in that order (Whitacre, 2007) as explained below:

Answering Behavioral Questions with STAR

Situation Provides the general context of the situation and your position. What was the specific environment and people involved in a particular process? What were the goals that the organization or you tried to achieve? Why were those goals important?

Task Clearly states the goal you wish to achieve, thereby identifying an issue. Is a process not working as expected? Are there undesirable outcomes to a decision? Is a goal not being accomplished? It is important to remember to use neutral language when you identify a task (i.e., say issue instead of problem).

Action Describes an intervention taken. What did you do first? And then what?

Result Provides a measurable improvement or change accomplished by your intervention. Sometimes the result can involve a lesson learned, particularly if you describe a failure.

The key to a good STAR answer is to bring in all four elements and provide enough specifics that the interviewer understands the story but not so much detail that they lose the point or the skill you want to show. To demonstrate effective use of STAR, I have reproduced several statements that Sociology students developed in answer to a question about their greatest skills. Notice that each example tries to keep a conversational tone to avoid sounding stilted or mechanical.

I recommend that you begin by thinking about the action you took, then move backwards to recount the situation and the issue elements, before moving forward to reveal the result. For example, one of my students had an internship evaluating the outcomes of a program for youth development. During her internship, she developed a game of charades so that students could identify their emotions. Depending on what skill she wanted to emphasize, she can provide different stories. She wanted to emphasize both creativity and critical thinking skills. The context of the situation was a goal to develop emotional intelligence skills in teenaged students. They wanted to teach them how to identify and name their emotions. The issue was that the original activity, which had attempted to get them to describe their emotions individually, had not worked. Students felt uncomfortable and were distracted. The group charade exercise provided humor and levity as well as a competitive incentive to name the right emotion. The result was that the goal was achieved and the students had fun in the process. Another result was learning how to use humor and competition to improve group dynamics. Her final statement for the STAR answer was:

> *My internship was about evaluating and improving student engagement in a youth program. For example, one activity required that my group talk with our mentees individually about identifying and feeling emotions. The first time we did this it was difficult to keep the attention of our mentees and make them excited about the activity. I suggested a competitive charades-like game that involved all the mentees. The revision was that every person was to write down an emotion on a piece of paper and put it in a pile. Then, we each chose from the pile and acted out the emotion without using words or sounds. Whoever guessed the emotion correctly was given a point. The game was a success, as I was able to keep their attention and ensure they had fun while still developing emotional skills. From this experience, I learned that fun activities could overcome anxiety.*

Any action you took can be the source of a STAR answer to a question, and the words can be adjusted to fit several skills. For example, the previous description could have emphasized the teamwork she showed when she consulted her instructors for an alternative activity. By the same token, the description may imply that she helped guide the instructors through change, which would demonstrate leadership. You have almost limitless options in how you frame your situation. The process of taking an action and constructing a story around it, making it your story, is a very personal task.

I cannot tell you exactly how to do it. However, I can offer you some examples of what Sociology students have developed to highlight various skills.

Mentoring/Training/Communication Skills

> *At the restaurant I work for, I trained new employees. Because of my training experience, I have realized that every individual has their own way of learning. I make sure to incorporate all teaching styles in my training: audio, visual, and kinetic. An example of this is that whenever I am training individuals, I make sure to say every step aloud, demonstrate what I was talking about, and make sure the trainee has some time to also go through the process of what they are being trained on by themselves. This technique of layering communication/information channels has led to an increase in my success. Employees learn faster, and many of them become stellar employees in an industry with lots of turnover.*

Answering Behavioral Questions with STAR

Flexibility/Communication Skills

It was my responsibility as an Orientation Leader to advocate for my students' needs, facilitate productive group conversation, and customize the orientation experience according to the specific personalities and needs of my group. It was up to me to take their history and concerns into account when advising them on what their future at DePaul looked like, changing the themes and order of activities. Within each group, there were up to 20 students. Each student brought different experiences to the table, and they all had different concerns. Some students may be more interested in learning about the social aspects of college, while others have more questions about the academics. It was my job to reconcile these differences and find ways to address all their interests in an engaging manner. That way you reduce student anxiety.

Teamwork/Negotiation/Critical Thinking Skills

For restaurants to be able to reduce food waste, first they must track its sources. I was tasked with creating an effective way to keep track of food waste for my restaurant. My job was difficult because co-workers had different ideas about the ideal system. One of my co-workers wanted to track the waste weekly while the other wanted it daily. I took everyone's opinions and created a spreadsheet that met the goal of the project while also incorporating the ideas of my fellow employees. I decided for us to only do daily tracking for the more expensive waste products, while the other products were on a weekly schedule. This project was conducted effectively, and it is still used in tracking waste at the restaurant. I found that letting people voice their opinions not only improves team dynamics but produces better solutions.

Leadership/Training/Ethics Skills

Last year, I transferred Kroger store locations because I moved into the city after four years at a suburban location. I worked at the Starbucks inside the store, and because of the double affiliation, procedures can be unclear. I wanted to ensure that my team would feel secure without my in-person guidance and could continue their work without disruption. I decided that my best contribution would be to formalize procedures. I authored a new, comprehensive task list for the opening, mid, and closing shifts. I produced this checklist on my own time. A good leader is proactive and takes care of their subordinates and workers. My sister, who works at my old store and whom I trained before I left, tells me they still use my list daily.

Detail/Organizational Skills

As a nutrition aide in a kitchen hospital, I composed meal plans for 200 patients. I needed to formulate each plan to the specifications of doctors and dieticians. Doctors, nurses, and dieticians hand-write instructions in a hurry and therefore there is always a potential for errors. I meticulously analyzed patient nutrition charts for abnormalities or potential mistakes. Given my position, I could not create a more efficient system; the second-best thing was to make sure my process had enough control moments to ensure patient safety. I wanted to detect errors as soon as possible. The key to a well-organized process is creating a flow chart detailing when tasks are supposed to begin and finish with specific control points. Because of the importance and complexity of dietary needs, I always double-checked my work before submitting it. If a mistake arose, I made sure to correct the issue and take responsibility for my error. I could not avoid mistakes, but I made sure to correct them as soon as possible and the errors were never repeated.

As an intern for the US Department of State, I was tasked with assembling a database to track voting records by members of an organization dedicated to eliminate chemical weapons. I was given no system or specific instructions. I decided to create my own system, starting with using descriptive labels for files and keeping an extensive diary of data documents and variables. Because of my organization, I created a coherent set of data sources useful for future research.

Dealing with Difficult or Tricky Questions

Most of the questions in an interview are general in nature. They are also phrased in a positive way that allows you to concentrate on selling your best self. There are, however, a subset of questions that I would classify as difficult or tricky and that can create higher levels of anxiety.

The Negative Question

The most common formulation for a negative question is either being asked to name your weaknesses or talk about an occasion when you made a mistake and what you did afterwards. These questions are tricky since you still need to maintain

Dealing with Difficult or Tricky Questions

positive language while you explain your role in negative situations. These questions are designed to detect Type A personalities. If you have ever seen an episode of the TV show, *The Apprentice*, when Donald Trump was the host, whenever a losing team was brought into the boardroom, the meeting became a competition in blaming each other for the loss. Whoever accepted fault, for any reason, was fired. Donald Trump is the archetypal Type A personality: someone who does not accept mistakes by himself or others. While this attitude is popular in a few organizations and industries, most managers know that such an attitude creates a toxic work environment. Some people decide to answer this question with a "non-answer" or mention a weakness that is not really a weakness. They say that "they care too much" or are "too responsible." This kind of answer does not trick interviewers; they know that you are dodging the question. Interviewers are looking for real weaknesses with narratives of redemption. That means they are asking you to recognize a real weakness in yourself that can negatively affect your performance. But they also want to hear how you have learned to overcome that weakness. It is okay if your weakness requires constant vigilance if you have a good strategy to control it. For this question, I will use my own personal example below.

> *While I consider myself bilingual, I started learning English late, at 13 years old. Much of my English comes not from reading the classics of literature, but from television. This history has affected my writing. While I am good at content and clarity, my grammar is not as polished as I would like it to be. This weakness has taught me that it is okay to let go of my ego and rely on the help of my co-workers. After doing as much as I can to polish my writing, I ask my native-speaker colleagues, and sometimes pay students, to take a good look before I submit anything for publication. Of course, I also offer those who help me assistance for their projects, from content readings to Spanish translations. We are all stronger when we work together.*

The answer reveals genuine vulnerability. You may know how much we academics pride ourselves on our independent work and writing styles. However, it also highlights my language skills and teamwork. I do not recommend, however, that you describe a weakness related to the main skills wanted for the job you are seeking. With an answer like this, I would not be able to get a job as a copy editor, but for other jobs, it would not be damaging.

The other usual form of the negative question asks you to talk about a moment of failure or a mistake. You can use a similar answer. Instead of just mentioning a general skill, provide a specific moment where your weakness became a problem. Then describe how you either fixed that mistake and/or made sure it never happened again. Whatever form the negative question takes, the one thing you should never do is blame others for the situation or issue. Negative questions measure your capacity to be accountable and self-aware.

The "Do You Have Any Questions for Me?" Moment

I personally hate this question, usually posed at the end of the interview. I have always been tempted to answer, "I need a job, you have a job, what else is there to say?" I hope at this point I do not have to explain how monumentally wrong this answer would be, even if completely honest. To answer "no" may be interpreted as a lack of real interest or passion. This is a moment when you can highlight a bit of your research into the organization by asking them to expand on a particular point you read about. Do not overdo it, however: you want to show interest, not arrogance. Select something real, but a topic that allows the interviewer to provide you with a positive answer. Some potential examples might be:

- Can you tell me about the performance evaluation process used for this position?
- What is the main communication style in your organization/department?
- Can you give me an example of how the company follows X value?
- I noticed that the company has a Foundation. Does it offer employees opportunities to participate?
- What is your policy about remote work?

The COVID Question

Asking how you used your "free time" during the pandemic is the newest interview question. While understandably annoying, it provides an example of the positive bias in managerial and Human Resources framing. Leave it to them to assume that you should have been productive or acquired new skills during the worst disruption in social and work life since World War II. While our sociological selves may cringe at this question, you need to prepare a positive answer. Obviously, it is better if your answer includes a skill relevant to the position. Lacking that, you can always talk about time with family, mental health management, exercise, or any other socially acceptable way of spending free time.

Questions About Salary Expectations

I particularly hated this question at the beginning of my working life when I had little information about wages. Although not every place or interviewer will ask you this, it is better to be prepared. There are several different strategies that you may follow:

- Avoid naming a specific number. You can try to defer to the interviewer and ask them what the range for the position in their organization is. This is the strategy most recommended by career advisors. However, you will eventually need to negotiate salaries, so the rest of the strategies described here can be used after you have received a job offer.
- Some job descriptions offer a specific number. In that case, remind the interviewer of that fact and ask if there has been any change.
- Some job descriptions provide a range, in which case I would think of how you stack up compared to other candidates. For example, if you are an exceptional candidate, I would mention a number around 80% of the maximum. If you are qualified but inexperienced, mention a number around 20% above the minimum. Remember, women and minorities tend to underestimate their skills, so try to account for that when deciding on what number to name.
- You can find information online for ranges of starting salaries in particular jobs or industries. You can then mention the range. You can also estimate a desired amount using the percentages method described in the previous point.
- You might consult your contacts, including those online, to see if anybody can give you more specific information about salaries in that organization or for that position.

After you have finished each interview, you need to email at least the lead person in the process to thank them for their work and attention. You should also mention a positive anecdote that happened during the interview. You want to reinforce that memory as well as the interviewer's positive emotions.

Assessing the Employer

I have concentrated on how to approach the process of managing impressions during the interview process. You can also use the interview to see if the position and the organization are a good fit for you. I do not recommend going into the interview with the attitude that you are "testing" the organization. Likewise, avoid reacting negatively to information you learn in the moment, during the interview. You can "debrief" your performance and the environment of the organization afterwards with a friend or mentor. You should also take a few minutes to reflect on your feelings about the position based on the information your received. If and when you get an offer, this information becomes relevant. Depending on your personal or financial needs, you may decide to turn down an offer if you think it is not a good fit. Not every opportunity is the right opportunity. Part of the application ritual is the mutual understanding that companies may not extend offers and candidates may not accept them. If you decide to reject an offer, be courteous, careful, and do not offer any negative opinions about the organization. It is never good to burn bridges.

Conclusion

The selection process is formed by a variety of scaffolded tests and interviews that attempt to measure your future job performance. Organizations commonly use cognitive and personality tests, but the profile of the successful candidate depends on the culture of the organization and the type of job. There is not a lot of opportunity to prepare or plan for tests. On the other hand, interviews, which are always part of the process, require extensive preparation. They are very standardized and hierarchical rituals. Success in the interview process depends on fulfilling the expectations of the employer. While there are dozens of potential questions, the format of the responses is very standard. Regardless of the questions, avoid using negative language. Utilizing knowledge about the organization and the position, you should use the STAR system to prepare answers that display your skills. This system offers a way to organize a story in four elements: Situation, Task, Action, and Result. You can adapt it to provide similar answers to different questions. Exercise care in answering difficult or negative questions.

Discussion Questions

1. What part or element of the selection process creates the most anxiety for you?
2. What is your sociological opinion of tests as a selection tool? Should they be eliminated or continued? Think of the effect of tests on individual applicants, on the organization, and on society in general.

3. Are personality traits biological or social? Is there a difference among personality dimensions (extroversion, conscientiousness, neuroticism, agreeableness, and openness) in their biological or social nature? For example, is extroversion determined more by biology and conscientiousness more by culture?
4. Are there any specific elements of your habitus that need to be transformed or developed for the workplace?
5. Read all the STAR statements. Which one do you think is the best? Why?
6. Read all the STAR statements. How would you improve them?

Action/Reflection Activity

1. What are your three strongest skills? Create a STAR system example for each. At least one of them should be a NACE skill/competence described in Chap. 6.
2. What is your greatest weakness in the context of your professional life? Using the STAR system, provide an example of how you overcame that weakness.
3. Provide an example where you made a mistake and what steps you took after realizing it. Use the STAR system to describe your learning process.
4. What activity or goal did you develop during the pandemic? Use the STAR system to describe the experience.

Works Cited

Heine, S. J., et al. (2008). What do cross-national comparisons of personality traits tell us? The case of conscientiousness. *Psychological Science, 19*(4), 309–313.

Meisenhelder, T. (2006). From character to habitus in sociology. *The Social Science Journal, 43*(1), 55–66.

Meyer, J. W., & Rowan, B. (1977). Institutionalized organizations: Formal structure as myth and ceremony. *American Journal of Sociology, 83*(2), 340–363.

Morrison, K. A. (1997). Personality correlates of the five-factor model for a sample of business owners/managers: Associations with scores on self-monitoring, Type A behavior, locus of control, and subjective well-being. *Psychological Reports, 80*(1), 255–272.

Ones, D. S., Viswesvara, C., & Dilcher, S. (2005). Cognitive ability in selection decisions. In *Handbook of understanding and measuring intelligence* (pp. 431–468). Sage Publications.

Parsons, T. (1958). Social structure and the development of personality: Freud's contribution to the integration of psychology and sociology. *Psychiatry, 21*(4), 321–340.

Pickel, A. (2005). The habitus process: A biopsychosocial conception. *Journal for the Theory of Social Behaviour, 35*(4), 437–461.

Riska, E. (2000). The rise and fall of Type A man. *Social Science & Medicine, 51*(11), 1665–1674.

Vinchur, A. J., & Bryan, L. L. K. (2012). A history of personnel selection and assessment. *The Oxford Handbook of Personnel Assessment and Selection*, 31–47.

Whetzel, D. L., et al. (2010). Linearity of personality–performance relationships: A large-scale examination. *International Journal of Selection and Assessment, 18*(3), 310–320.

Whitacre, T. (2007). Behavioral interviewing-find your STAR. *Quality Progress, 40*(6), 72.

From Jobs to Careers 12

When I was a college student in Mexico, my university celebrated its first 50th anniversary. To mark the occasion, it held a series of conferences featuring world leaders. One of these guest speakers was the CEO of Citibank at the time. I've forgotten his name, but I remember his career advice to us students who were about to graduate. He was talking about his own career, how he did his work to the best of his ability, and then won promotions. His implicit message was that if you are good enough, the only career management you will need is to work hard. I was thankful that the event was virtual and out of sight. To see how hard I was rolling my eyes, he would have felt deeply insulted.

Even as a green, inexperienced undergraduate student, I had no doubt that such claims were false. I did not believe that hard work and talent were enough to ensure an exceptional career, not even for people in the United States. My many subsequent years of sociological training have confirmed that he was recalling his career through rose-colored glasses. Or to be more precise and sociological, he was looking through white-male-elite-colored glasses. Career management requires more than hard work.

I've mentioned key issues regarding career management previously in this book. Networking and community-building are the cornerstones of career development. Being able to advocate for yourself and adapt to the language of organizations is another essential tool. While job search and application protocols are a central part of career management, particularly in the transition from school to work, you will face other complex issues as you progress through your career. The road to personal and professional fulfillment is complicated and will be different for everybody. Career management is one of those areas that involves permanent learning. I will conclude my advice on employability and career management with a discussion of three recommendations for how to: (1) manage your job expectations, particularly when it comes to authenticity, (2) maintain healthy boundaries through resistance, and (3) prevent fear from hindering your job mobility.

Manage Your Expectations: Authenticity and Decoupling

As a new worker, you will surely have expectations that do not fit the reality of the work environment. When I found my first job, I asked someone how to request your birthday off. I still remember the incredulous look I got. At that time in Mexico, that was something a good worker would not do. This particular example does not apply to modern US workplace norms which offer more flexibility in the use of PTO (paid time off) and where employees can and should use them to their advantage. However, some organizations provide no paid vacation during an employee's first year of work, no sick time, and may try to control when and why you take time off. This is an aspect of the organization worth investigating before you accept an offer—but only after the job offer is made.

You will find many culture shocks as you start your career and move from one organization to another. A major source of conflict will be expectations of authenticity. Both outside and inside academic settings, the normative value of authenticity has gained prominence in the twenty-first century. At its most basic, think of authenticity as a "form of alignment of one's internal sense of self (e.g., beliefs, values, motivations) and the external expression of it" (Hewlin et al., 2020). This definition suggests a lack of hypocrisy, which is indeed considered a modern sin. In academia, however, the issue of authenticity is not about hypocrisy but "fakeness." Used in this sense, the concern is how to maintain the "authenticity" of artifacts (content, relationships, experiences) in the presence of modern forces, mainly technology and capitalism (Pérez, 2019). This line of discussion surrounding authenticity started in the early 2000s with studies on the possibility of authentic religious experiences through mediated and online content (Radde-Antweiler, 2013). It has also been extended to issues related to capitalism through an emerging line of research focused on authentic tourism (Chhabra, 2005) and brand marketing (Nunes et al., 2021).

Authenticity confronts Sociology students in two ways. The first involves your desire to be accepted and embraced for the identities you both inherit and create for yourself. A good definition for this issue comes from Kernis and Goldman (2006) who define authenticity as "the unobstructed operation of one's true- or core-self in one's daily enterprise." Organizations vary considerably in the degree to which they accept diverse identities. For students, values related to gender, sexual orientation, race, and ethnicity usually arouse the most concern. Being able to bring and display these identities in the workplace without fear of negative consequences is a non-negotiable job requirement. However, Sociology students are looking for more than mere accommodation: they want their identities to be understood and celebrated.

The second aspect of authenticity that students often grapple with involves transparency. As sociologists, you want organizations to recognize the problems they themselves create. Current management theories hold diversity (racial, ethnic, gender, and intellectual) as a positive value. Students expect organizations to at least fulfill the social obligations they have already promised in their mission and values statements, including those within their marketing and public relations messages. In keeping with the principles of the human relations school and other socio-emotional management techniques, they want such principles to be "real" rather than just discourse.

The activities you did in Parts I and II of this book will help you develop a feeling of authenticity. Identity Integration (i.e., integrating your personal and sociological selves) is a pre-condition to feeling authentic in your career (Ebrahimi et al., 2020). Individuals feel more authentic when their home and work identities overlap. Authentic people behave ethically. Authenticity in the workplace has limits. Asking authenticity of organizations can invite disappointment. Organizations are not likely to be receptive to identities that interfere with their mission and their levels of control. They are also likely to abandon their commitments to those identities if they create vulnerabilities with other stakeholders. The identity demands of employees and investors, for example, tend to be in conflict. You cannot expect organizations to keep strong levels of commitments to all their policies. Understanding organizational dynamics requires you to recognize that in the presence of multiple and conflicting demands from stakeholders (investors, government, employees, community, professional organizations), organizations use a strategy of decoupling (Meyer & Rowan, 1977). This strategy entails "formally (and publicly) adopting a given policy, procedure or program without actually implementing it" (MacLean et al., 2015). In other words, organizations say many things, but do not necessarily follow through.

Decoupling strategies are embedded in managerial techniques. Sometimes they are inadvertently deployed, such as in how managers can refer to workers both as assets or as liabilities depending on the context, ignoring this inherent contradiction. Sometimes it is done on purpose, as a form of framing an issue to elicit collective action (Goffman, 1974; Manning, 2008). Positive framing, an aspect of business language discussed previously in this book, is a form of decoupling: if a problem is not recognized, there is no obligation to fix it. Decoupling is not necessarily done with the intent of doing harm or purposely lying; it is part of the social fiction of daily organizational life. It is difficult for organizations and individuals to fulfill all the high and varied standards of our era, especially considering the lack of agreement on values, priorities, or how to implement them. In this context, decoupling is a rational response to complexity.

On average, organizations are getting better at accepting a variety of identities in the workplace. The very presence of a greater variety of identities in society has consequences for the composition of labor markets. Outside of extremely specific occupations and industries (i.e., STEM and technology), diversity is the norm rather than the exception. As for the "realness" of managerial discourse, I am more skeptical. Research on authentic leadership is taking place (Gardner et al., 2011), but with decoupling so entrenched in organizational behavior, an embrace of authentic leadership practices is limited. Although some individual managers view authentic leadership as an asset in their work, managers in general are not trained in the kind of self-reflective analysis that would lead them in that direction.

If decoupling is the norm in work organizations, then one solution is to decouple back. As an individual, you can participate in the fictions of the organization without necessarily believing them yourself. Or you can even believe them but recognize their limits. Most of us do not go about our lives telling people what they are doing wrong. Sometimes we fib to make people feel better. As long as all the participants are aware of the obfuscation, decoupling is useful and harmless. It becomes a strategy for avoiding conflict.

As a Sociology teacher, however, I would like you to reflect on the social consequences of our search for authenticity. The concept is very egocentric in the sense that it puts the self before the social, a traditional Western bias. In our modern world, authenticity is always questioned and must be proved constantly (Bai et al., 2020). One of my students did a wonderful paper on how the label of "depressed," once a stigma, is now a source of social status. The problem, however, is that such social status is only conferred on the "authentically" depressed, whatever that may mean. I want you to consider that, just maybe, we do not need to impose such harsh standards on ourselves and others. We can just live, however we like, without having to justify our choices to anyone, ourselves included. And we can extend that grace to our co-workers and managers.

Maintain Healthy Boundaries: The Art of Resistance

Organizational and managerial cultures, with their emphasis on control through both externalized and internalized mechanisms, have often been compared to a religion or a cult. If we take organizational discourse seriously, the organization wants your body, your mind, and your soul. Such far-reaching demands take on a sinister note when you consider the serious imbalance of power between employer and employee. Government regulation tempers that imbalance by putting limits on what organizations can and cannot do in the workplace. In the United States, federal regulations provide a minimum or floor that applies to the nation. These federal regulations concerning worker-employee relations are rather minimal. They recognize that employees have a right to take sick time off, but it can be unpaid. Similarly, the federal minimum wage is low. Individual states can enact their own legislation that may complement or augment federal regulations. The character and level of protection they afford workers will depend on the states' political leanings, both historic and current, and their legislatures. Similarly, the enforcement of federal legislation, particularly related to unionization, varies significantly depending on the political party occupying the White House. Finally, supreme courts, both federal and state, play a crucial role in determining the constitutionality of labor policies, laws, and practices. Sociology graduates, just like any other worker in the United States, will have to deal with a complex and contradictory system with varying degrees of enforcement. I recommend that as a new worker you should research your state's labor-related legislation and see what specific policies the HR Department in your organization follows.

Employers are allowed to monitor you if they have a business-related reason to do so or if they have your consent. Given how broad the first condition is, employers in effect can monitor you the entire time in which you are working or present in the workspace, which nowadays may include your home. This right extends from reading your email to videotaping you while working and tracking your use of company websites and software packages, among many other forms of surveillance. For all practical purposes, privacy does not exist in the workplace. You should always be aware that the company may be monitoring you.

Beyond government regulations and their enforcement, the best mechanism for ensuring worker protection is unions, which serve as a collective counterpart to the power of organizations. Few if any positions that attract Sociology graduates are union jobs. By definition, managers are legally and ethically obligated to uphold the interests of their organizations. They are forbidden from joining unions to avoid a conflict of interest to their fiduciary duties. Participating in collective action and exercising your right to free speech, although technically protected by law, opens you to potential retaliation by your employer.

Besides legal rights and union membership, you also have the capacity for meaningful action in how you maintain boundaries. Resistance, both passive and active, is always an option. Hodson (1995) describes four types of resistance: (1) deflecting abuse, (2) regulating the amount and intensity of work, (3) defending worker autonomy, and (4) expanding worker control. As a worker, you are an active, creative participant in the life of the organization. Your discursive consciousness (Giddens, 1979) allows you to co-opt organizational forms of control to your benefit (Mathieu, 2009). You have discursive strategies at your disposal for deflecting managerial control, including the use of irony (Sewell, 2008), humor and joking (Westwood & Johnston, 2013), "bitching" and gossip (Sotirin & Gottfried, 1999), mimicry (Dey & Teasdale, 2016), and many others.

These strategies all signal a certain lack of consent without directly challenging authority. To me, they are more sophisticated forms of decoupling than those practiced by most employers. These are decoupling strategies for those who are in a vulnerable position. They depend on social norms regarding what can and cannot be said and done on the job. Helpfully, some forms of resistance also have positive organizational consequences, like aiding socialization (Ribarsky & Hammonds, 2019), dealing with controversial issues (Kwon et al., 2020), and coping with change (Wallace & Hoyle, 2012). Engaging in the game of decoupling with your managers is a form of socially acceptable passive resistance. There are more examples of active resistance, specifically during service delivery, such as the "seat belt squeeze" reportedly utilized to punish obnoxious riders at Disneyland (Van Maanen & Kunda, 1989), clerks' withholding their smiles when lines are too long (Sutton & Rafaeli, 1988), and customer service representatives hanging up on callers in ways that management cannot track (Van Den Broek, 2002).

But be careful not to overromanticize resistance as part of your sociological identity (Kondo, 1990). Your relationship with your employer is adversarial (Geertz, 1992). The word adversarial does not mean that you are necessarily competing with your boss or in permanent conflict, but that the fundamental goals of the working relationship are different for employers and workers. Yet, at the same time, workers and employers need each other. Your employer needs you to perform the work, and you need the employer to provide a job. The goals of employer and employee are not in direct contradiction but loosely opposite. The trick to resistance is to achieve a certain level of boundary maintenance without irreparably breaking the relationship. If you push too much or too obviously, resistance has consequences. Overt resistance is punished by organizations. The behavior of your professors is not a good guide for practicing successful resistance in the workplace.

A lot of the resistance practices that your professors engage in inside and outside the classroom would be severely punished in most other organizational settings. Even faculty get punished for their resistance, maybe not by losing our jobs if we have tenure, but by being labeled "crazy" or "out of touch" by other departments in universities. There is no single best way to resist. The right form of resistance depends on the specific control strategy you are trying to resist (Hodson, 1995).

Resistance is complicated and requires subtlety. You will have to establish your own dividing line between cooperating and resisting. Whatever you do, do not fall for managerial discourse that labels resistance as unethical. If the organization is asking you to do things that are not part of a balanced economic transaction, you need to resist. Take, for example, the warning heard from many managers (one happily going out of style thanks to salary-posting websites like Salary.com and Glassdoor) against sharing your salary information with anybody. Your silence in issues of money only benefits the organization. The same standard applies to ethical violations, fraud, or discrimination.

Avoid Fear: Job Mobility and the Crises of Capitalism

Conservatives on labor often point out that if a job is bad or underpaid, a worker has a right to leave, which they consider enough protection from abuse. Of course, outright slavery and indentured servitude are illegal in America. However, some bosses have been found to pressure workers to remain longer than they want by guilting them or even refusing to accept resignations. As a worker, you do not owe an organization anything beyond a two-week notice of your resignation. It is a sad state of affairs if the only thing to recommend a job is that you can leave it, but the strength inherent within the *power* of leaving is real. That means that your willingness and ability to engage in job mobility give you some power. It is not uncommon for companies to only offer a promotion or a raise when an employee informs them of an alternative offer. I have seen companies promise promotions in exchange for additional education or skills training only to renege once the employee reaches the agreed-upon milestone. Other organizations simply do not negotiate or oppose your decision to leave. In the end, we are all replaceable; the leverage of another job offer is limited. Regardless, being open to the idea of quitting is an important aspect of career management.

The likelihood that you or any other worker will engage in job mobility depends on three types of factors: (1) dispositional attributes that affect one's preference for change, (2) decisions related to specific situations, and (3) macro-level conditions that affect the availability of positions (Ng et al., 2007). In terms of dispositions, aspirations are an important element, as is a personal propensity for boredom or adventure (Van Vianen et al., 2003). Situational factors refer to a comparison between your satisfaction with your current job and the attractiveness of alternative offers (Morris & Villemez, 1992). Low job satisfaction is a problem best solved by looking for better opportunities. What you want to avoid at all costs is to fall into an "anti-mobility" subculture in which you and your co-workers adapt to lack of opportunity by avoiding responsibility and maintaining low performance (Kanter, 2008). Getting trapped in such a subculture has negative effects on your career.

As an economic sociologist, I have more expertise and interest in the macro-level conditions affecting job availability. We know that economic conditions during their early years (childhood, adolescence, labor market entrance) affect people's perceptions of their career mobility and intergenerational mobility (Gugushvili, 2021). My students often complain to me that they got trapped between the Great Recession and the COVID-19 pandemic and now are waiting for another recession to hit.

I cannot disagree with this perception. Capitalism is riddled with many types of crises. There are crises of overproduction. These crises used to be about how a reduction in demand and an accumulation of inventory led manufacturers to reduce operations and lay off workers. Crises of overproduction have become less common with the introduction of new managerial techniques like Just-in-Time in which suppliers only send production goods when needed, reducing inventories to a minimum. The tendency of public organizations to pay too much attention to Wall Street can create other crises. When companies reduce their workforces, Wall Stret rewards them with increases in stock valuation whether or not excess personnel contributed to the problem being addressed. If the problem is unrelated to labor issues, eventually the company will respond with new rounds of hiring. The same scenario happens when a recession is predicted. For example, at the start of the pandemic many companies reduced their labor forces in anticipation of an economic crisis that never quite materialized. Now they are facing labor shortages and must hire new workers at higher salaries or find no workers at all. These cycles are more pronounced in the for-profit sector, but they also exist among nonprofits.

Some crises are due to irrational exuberance, a term coined by former Federal Reserve Chair Alan Greenspan in the 1990s and first used to warn people about the dot-com bubble of the 2000s. It refers to how unduly optimistic assessments of current and future economic conditions can lead to an increase in asset valuations driven by over-confident investors. While originally a financial term, its use has expanded to include consumer behaviors like those related to residential housing markets. When something eventually happens to prove that optimism ill-founded, asset prices plunge. We normally call these crises "bubbles" (Carruthers, 2009).

Bubbles tend to affect job creation, first by increasing demand for workers and then by suddenly dropping demand when companies go bankrupt or decide to downsize. The technology industry is in a permanent state of irrational exuberance with high stock valuations and low profits or contracting workforces. As I write this, companies like PayPal, Microsoft, Spotify, IBM, and Alphabet have announced plans to cut thousands of positions within the year (Rogers, 2023). In general, new industries tend to overpromise, and when they cannot deliver on expectations, their market value suffers. Yet, no matter how often our expectations are proven wrong, we seem unable to prevent irrational exuberance.

Two additional categories of crises originate outside the sphere of economic markets, and concern natural and political occurrences. Natural crises could be called "acts of God," except that they always involve a lack of government regulation or deficient intervention. Although governments cannot control mother nature, they can mitigate its impact. This type of crisis includes the COVID-19 pandemic, natural disasters like hurricanes and floods, environmental degradation and pollution, or global warming. Political crises are directly created by governments. Any change in government regulation can spark or precipitate an adjustment in the economy, but drastic policies create bigger crises. For example, the war between Russia and Ukraine is affecting the world's food supply, and animosity between the United States and China is disrupting commodity chains in many industries, contributing to inflation.

Every generation has crises that affect their prospects and their character. Baby boomers were traumatized by the oil and inflation crises of the 1970s. Gen X dealt with potential nuclear Armageddon, difficult market prospects brought on by early global outsourcing of jobs, and the dot-com bust. Millennials had to deal with the long aftermath of 9/11, and many graduated just in time to face the aftermath of the financial crisis. I am not mentioning this to make you afraid of all the potential macro factors that can affect your job prospects. On the contrary, despite this penchant for courting crises, we still go on with our lives and careers. No crisis lasts forever, at least not in the United States.

Depending on the crisis, certain sectors of the economy are negatively affected while others continue as normal. Crises even produce new opportunities in certain industries. For instance, think of how the COVID-19 pandemic set off a boom in the furniture industry. The same crisis which everybody predicted would diminish worker opportunities helped generate one of the most worker-favorable labor markets in the last 30 years. This improved labor market was partly caused by the widespread defection of workers who left their jobs to seek more satisfying alternatives.

Fear is the biggest obstacle to upward job mobility—fear of developing a negative-looking career record, fear of reprisal, fear of not finding a better opportunity, fear of making a mistake, or fear of the unknown. Job mobility is a requirement for good career management. The US Bureau of Labor Statistics (2021) estimates that baby boomers (those born between 1946 and 1964) held on average 5.6 different jobs from ages 18–24. The same baby boomers had an average 12.4 jobs during the period when they were 18 to 54 years old. We know there are variations between cohorts in job mobility, but conventional wisdom seems to indicate that this current cohort of those newly entering the job market will have higher job turnover than baby boomers. These numbers may suggest how much job-changing you might expect over your lifetime. If you have gone through the activities in this book, you now have evidence that you are a talented person trained in a rigorous discipline with skills valued by the marketplace. You are ready to find and forge your own place in the world of work.

Conclusion

Career management is an ongoing activity that requires continuous learning and attention to your environment inside and outside the organization. This chapter offered three final pieces of advice for navigating your career by managing your expectations of authenticity, maintaining healthy boundaries through resistance, and approaching job mobility without fear. Sociology students crave authenticity, both a desire to bring your personal identities to work with you and to join organizations whose words and actions are in alignment with yours. However, it would be wise to recognize that because most organizations engage in decoupling, their commitment to authenticity will be limited. Since organizations aim to control and ensure worker loyalty, workers need to learn how to develop and maintain healthy boundaries from organizational expectations. Different resistance strategies, like gossip, humor, and irony, are socially acceptable ways you can use to help maintain boundaries. A final tool of career management is job mobility. While your personal disposition and situational aspects can affect your likelihood of changing jobs, your perception of macro factors also has an effect. In particular, the ubiquity of crises and crisis narratives creates fear of change. Avoid excessive fear related to job mobility if you want to achieve your personal best and your career goals.

Discussion Questions

1. What are your expectations about bringing your personal identity to future workplaces?
2. What is more important for a good workplace: the ability to bring your personal identity to work or the alignment of an employer's language and actions?
3. Can you think of instances in which you personally engage in something like organizational decoupling?
4. Think of the authority relationships in your life. Have you ever engaged in a form of resistance? Was it successful?
5. What form of resistance are you personally more comfortable with?
6. Which situations in the workplace do you think call for compliance and which for resistance?
7. How do you feel about current crises compared to those experienced by earlier generations? What would your sociological self say?
8. How does the idea of changing jobs make you feel?
9. Would you want to stay with the same organization all your life? What would be the negative consequences of such an option?

Action/Reflection Activity

1. Contact a Sociology alum in a job or organization that interests you.
2. Talk to them about their organizational environment, their policies related to the expression of personal identities, decoupling practices, and their policies and systems for supervising the work.
3. Write a three- or four-page reflection on the advantages and challenges you would likely face in this organization.

Works Cited

Bai, F., Ho, G. C. C., & Liu, W. (2020). Do status incentives undermine morality-based status attainment? Investigating the mediating role of perceived authenticity. *Organizational Behavior and Human Decision Processes, 158*, 126–138.

Bureau of Labor Statistics. (2021). TED: The Economics Daily: Baby boomers born from 1957 held average of 12.4 jobs from ages 18 to 54. Retrieved at https://www.bls.gov/opub/ted/2021/baby-boomers-born-from-1957-to-1964-held-an-average-of-12-4-jobs-from-ages-18-to-54.htm#:~:text=Bureau%20of%20Labor%20Statistics%2C%20U.S.%20Department%20of%20Labor%2C,to%2054%20at%20https%3A%2F%2Fwww.bls.

gov%2Fopub%2Fted%2F2021%2Fbaby-boomers-born-from-1957-to-1964-held-anaverage-of-12-4-jobs-from-ages-18-to-54.htm%20%28visited%20September%20 16%2C%202023%29 on September 25th, 2023.

Carruthers, B. G. (2009). A sociology of bubbles. *Contexts, 8*(3), 22–26.

Chhabra, D. (2005). Defining authenticity and its determinants: Toward an authenticity flow model. *Journal of Travel Research, 44*(1), 64–73.

Dey, P., & Teasdale, S. (2016). The tactical mimicry of social enterprise strategies: Acting 'as if' in the everyday life of third sector organizations. *Organization, 23*(4), 485–504.

Ebrahimi, M., Kouchaki, M., & Patrick, V. M. (2020). Juggling work and home selves: Low identity integration feels less authentic and increases unethicality. *Organizational Behavior and Human Decision Processes, 158*, 101–111.

Gardner, W. L., Cogliser, C. C., Davis, K. M., & Dickens, M. P. (2011). Authentic leadership: A review of the literature and research agenda. *The Leadership Quarterly, 22*(6), 1120–1145.

Geertz, C. (1992). The bazaar economy: Information and search in peasant marketing. *The Sociology of Economic Life*, 225–232.

Giddens, A. (1979). *Central problems in social theory: Action, structure and contradiction in social analysis*. Macmillan.

Goffman, E. (1974). *Frame analysis: An essay on the organization of experience*. Harvard University Press.

Gugushvili, A. (2021). Why do people perceive themselves as being downwardly or upwardly mobile? *Acta Sociologica, 64*(1), 3–23.

Hewlin, P. F., Karelaia, N., Kouchaki, M., & Sedikides, C. (2020). *Authenticity at work: Its shapes, triggers, and consequences* (Vol. 158, pp. 80–82). Elsevier.

Hodson, R. (1995). Worker resistance: An underdeveloped concept in the sociology of work. *Economic and Industrial Democracy, 16*(1), 79–110.

Kanter, R. M. (2008). *Men and women of the corporation: New edition*. Basic books.

Kernis, M. H., & Goldman, B. M. (2006). A multicomponent conceptualization of authenticity: Theory and research. *Advances in Experimental Social Psychology, 38*, 283–357.

Kondo, D. K. (1990). *Crafting selves: Power, gender, and discourses of identity in a Japanese workplace*. University of Chicago Press.

Kwon, W., Clarke, I., Vaara, E., Mackay, R., & Wodak, R. (2020). Using verbal irony to move on with controversial issues. *Organization Science, 31*(4), 865–886.

MacLean, T., Litzky, B. E., & Holderness, D. K. (2015). When organizations don't walk their talk: A cross-level examination of how decoupling formal ethics programs affects organizational members. *Journal of Business Ethics, 128*, 351–368.

Manning, P. K. (2008). Goffman on organizations. *Organization Studies, 29*(5), 677–699.

Mathieu, C. (2009). Practising gender in organizations: The critical gap between practical and discursive consciousness. *Management Learning, 40*(2), 177–193.

Meyer, J. W., & Rowan, B. (1977). Institutionalized organizations: Formal structure as myth and ceremony. *American Journal of Sociology, 83*(2), 340–363.

Morris, J. M., & Villemez, W. J. (1992). Mobility potential and job satisfaction: Mixing dispositional and situational explanations. *Work and Occupations, 19*(1), 35–58.

Ng, T. W., Sorensen, K. L., Eby, L. T., & Feldman, D. C. (2007). Determinants of job mobility: A theoretical integration and extension. *Journal of Occupational and Organizational Psychology, 80*(3), 363–386.

Works Cited

Nunes, J. C., Ordanini, A., & Giambastiani, G. (2021). The concept of authenticity: What it means to consumers. *Journal of Marketing, 85*(4), 1–20.

Pérez, A. (2019). Building a theoretical framework of message authenticity in CSR communication. *Corporate Communications: An International Journal.*

Radde-Antweiler, K. (2013). Authenticity. Digital religion: Understanding religious practice in new media worlds, 88–103.

Ribarsky, E., & Hammonds, J. (2019). Gossiping for the good of it? Examining the link between gossip and organizational socialization. *Kentucky Journal of Communication, 38*(1).

Rogers, J. (2023). More than 85,000 tech-sector employees have lost their jobs since the start of the year. MatrketWatch. Retrieved from https://www.msn.com/en-us/money/companies/more-than-82000-tech-sector-employees-have-lost-their-jobs-since-the-start-of-the-year/ar-AA16UPhV

Sewell, G. (2008). The fox and the hedgehog go to work: A natural history of workplace collusion. *Management Communication Quarterly, 21*(3), 344–363.

Sotirin, P., & Gottfried, H. (1999). The ambivalent dynamics of secretarialbitching': Control, resistance, and the construction of identity. *Organization, 6*(1), 57–80.

Sutton, R. I., & Rafaeli, A. (1988). Untangling the relationship between displayed emotions and organizational sales: The case of convenience stores. *Academy of Management Journal, 31*(3), 461–487.

Van Den Broek, D. (2002). Monitoring and surveillance in call centres: Some responses from Australian workers. *Labour & Industry: A Journal of the Social and Economic Relations of Work, 12*(3), 43–58.

Van Maanen, J., & Kunda, G. (1989). Real feelings. Emotional expression and organizational culture. In L. L. Cummings & B. M. Staw (Eds.), *Research in organizational behaviour* (Vol. 11). JAI Press.

Van Vianen, A. E., Feij, J. A., Krausz, M., & Taris, R. (2003). Personality factors and adult attachment affecting job mobility. *International Journal of Selection and Assessment, 11*(4), 253–264.

Wallace, M., & Hoyle, E. (2012). The dynamics of irony in organizational change: Coping with a school merger. *Public Administration, 90*(4), 974–999.

Westwood, R. I., & Johnston, A. (2013). Humor in organization: From function to resistance. *Humor, 26*(2), 219–247.

Index

A
Action
  orientations, 12, 23, 26–28, 32, 109, 112, 119–122, 136
  verbs, 121
Alumni, 7, 10, 39, 50, 58, 61, 62, 76, 77, 173
American Sociological Association (ASA), 6, 20, 35, 58, 112
Anxiety, 4, 9, 52, 55–56, 61, 62, 66, 70, 72, 75, 76, 82, 91, 99, 135, 143, 144, 150, 173, 174, 179, 180, 184
Applications, 11, 67–69, 81, 82, 89, 90, 95, 96, 102, 112, 119, 121, 133, 135, 136, 138, 143, 144, 149, 162, 169, 174, 176, 184, 187
Authenticity, 72, 188–190, 196

B
Bias
  class, 85
  gender, 85
  racial, 85, 120
Bourdieu, Pierre, 17, 41, 43, 73, 160

C
Capital
  cultural, 172
  human, 83, 161, 165
  social, 67–69, 76, 160
Capitalism
  effects, 158, 166
  profits, 156, 158
Community, 12, 18, 24, 27, 28, 30, 35, 38, 40–44, 49–63, 65, 67–69, 76, 88, 111, 119, 121, 123, 126, 128, 131, 135, 140, 145, 149, 150, 167, 175, 189
Competencies, NACE, 8, 104–109, 114, 119, 123, 125, 133, 185
Control, 8, 20, 29, 50, 54, 66, 71, 93, 119, 149, 157–160, 162, 164, 169, 180, 181, 188, 189, 191–193, 195, 196
Cover letter
  elements of, 145
  examples of, 145–149
COVID-19, 7, 55, 69, 74, 91, 137, 166, 170, 182, 185, 194, 195
Critical Theories (critical approaches), 44, 160

D
Decoupling, 121, 192, 196, 197
Durkheim, Emile, 38, 39, 44, 53

E
Education
  cost, 5
  purpose, 42
  quality, 4
  value, 8, 9
Efficiency, 83–85, 95, 125, 146, 156, 157, 160, 164, 166
Ethics, 30, 35–39, 46, 47, 138, 159, 165, 179–180
Exploitation, 22, 25, 27, 29, 43–45, 120, 161, 163–166

F
Frames/framing, 8, 55–56, 61, 109, 118–120, 125, 143, 174, 178, 182, 189

G
Guilt (or privilege), 30, 66

H
Heuristics, 24, 25, 29–32
Homophily, 51–52, 55, 61, 62, 67, 84
Human relations, school, 158–159, 175, 189
Human Resources, Department, 144, 159, 162, 165

I
Internships, 50, 57, 74, 75, 86, 117, 118, 126, 132, 135, 137–139, 141, 143, 150, 151, 155, 177
Interview
  informational, questions, 77
  script, answers, 72
  selection, questions, 169
  trick questions, 181

J
Jobs, 20, 22–24, 35, 37, 56, 57, 61, 62, 73, 77, 83, 85, 91, 93, 95, 99–102, 104, 109, 112–114, 123, 129–131, 138, 139, 144, 149, 171, 173, 175, 180, 182, 188, 190, 191
  communication, 126–127, 144
  education, 127–129
  general examples, 50, 118, 123
  hospitality, 124–126
  mobility, 66, 188, 193–196
  postings, 21, 88, 95, 101, 109–111, 120, 121, 137, 141, 144, 145, 147, 149, 150
  research, 149, 171
  retail, 123–124

L
Labor markets, 3, 10, 11, 13, 18, 54, 65, 67, 68, 82, 83, 99, 136, 137, 139, 161, 190, 194, 195
Language(s), 11, 13, 14, 36, 42, 81, 100–104, 109–111, 113, 114, 117–135, 143, 156, 171, 172, 174, 177, 181, 184, 187, 189, 197

M
Managers, 155
  attitudes, 181
  biases, 83, 182
  training, 155
Manipulation, 29, 156
Marx, Karl, 39, 43, 163
Mentor (or mentoring), 27, 32, 57, 58, 99, 118, 128, 178, 184
Meritocracy, 70–71
Minority (or minorities, minority-owned), 6, 39, 40, 42, 90, 137, 165–167, 183

N
National Association of Colleges and Employers (NACE), *see* Competencies, NACE
Neoliberalism, 4, 5, 7, 66, 158, 166

Index

Network/networking
  bonding, 67
  bridging, 67
  Internet/email, 68–70, 75
  scripts, 55, 72
  strangers, 54, 76
  strong ties, 69
Nonprofits, 5, 9, 27, 44, 59, 71, 91, 95, 119, 120, 139, 140, 145, 163–164, 166, 167, 170, 194
Normative knowledge, 37

P
Pandemic, see COVID-19
Positivism, 39
Productivity, 53, 76, 155, 157, 158, 165
Professionalism, 104
Professions
  career tracks, 21
  consecration, 21
  licensing, 21
  prestige, 21
  status, 19–21

R
Reciprocity, 51, 53–56, 61, 62, 74
Recruitment, see Selection process
Regulations, 161, 191, 195
Relationships
  expressive, 51–53, 55, 61, 62
  hybrid, 61
  instrumental, 53, 55, 61, 62
Research, see Jobs
Resistance, 84, 188–190, 196, 197
Resume
  elements, 83, 121
  examples, 95, 100
  functions, 83, 100, 121
  organization, 85, 89, 91, 110, 121, 150

S
Salary
  negotiating, 138, 183
  researching, 138

Scientific Management, 156–159, 163, 167
Selection process, 13, 67–70, 82, 143, 162, 169–185
Situation, Task, Action, Result (STAR), 169, 176–180, 184, 185
Skills
  language, 102–104, 113, 114, 171, 181
  socioemotional, 109–111, 114, 119, 123, 125, 145, 173
  technical, 97, 100–110, 113, 114, 119, 134, 145
  transferable, 11–13, 18, 81, 100, 101, 104–110, 113, 114, 118, 133, 136, 145, 169
Social boundaries, 52, 55, 56
Social capital
  bonding, 67
  bridging, 67
Social cohesion, 41, 44, 51
Social justice, 56, 61, 125
Social responsibility, 161
Sociological identity, 12, 22–23, 26, 30, 32, 46, 192
Sociological imagination, 13, 22, 23, 27, 41, 59, 156
Sociology/sociologists
  Code of Conduct, 36
  functions, 81, 83
  point of View, 12, 23, 24, 27, 99, 129
  status, 19–21
  types, 112
  vulnerabilities, 29–31

T
Tests, 81, 85, 91, 96, 103, 119, 169–173, 184

V
Value, College Degree, 4, 5, 7, 8
Values
  coordinated order, 38
  emancipation, 38–39
  truth, 37–38

W
Weber, Max, 26, 39, 45, 159, 160, 163

The manufacturer's authorised representative in the EU is Springer Nature Customer Service Centre GmbH, Europaplatz 3, 69115 Heidelberg, Germany. If you have any concerns regarding our products, please contact ProductSafety@springernature.com

Printed and bound by CPI Group (UK) Ltd, Croydon, CR0 4YY
23/03/2026
02076466-0002

"Increasing numbers of Sociology programs offer courses or sections of courses that focus on helping undergraduates prepare for careers. Martinez's The Employable Sociologist fills an important gap in the literature. It is distinctive because it focuses on the practical aspects of career development such as resume and cover letter writing, while providing critical insights from Economic Sociology to encourage Sociology students to reflect on career options in a capitalist society characterized by significant inequality and injustice."
—**Mary Scheuer Senter**, Professor of Sociology, Central Michigan University, USA

"This book takes a purpose-driven approach to providing practical solutions for navigating the job market. The author's clear and concise language, combined with relatable examples, makes complex concepts easily understandable. Each chapter builds upon the previous one, creating a clear path to follow toward a career. This book is written for students and parents without forsaking academic rigor. This must-have companion for Sociology majors should be a standard in Sociology departments worldwide."
—**Will Tyson**, Associate Professor, University of South Florida, USA

This book addresses a gap in and outside academia: how to help Sociology undergraduates develop skills for career success while maintaining a sociologically rigorous approach. Matching sociological theories, methods, and knowledge with contemporary capitalistic managerial and work practices, it shows how sociology undergraduates are not only employable but have marketable advantages over graduates of other disciplines. A student following the program embodied in this book will actively nurture a strong sociological identity; create a job search plan integrating personal and disciplinary interests, values, and skills; design job application materials that provide the best fit for specific jobs and organizations; and launch a satisfying career path. Beyond an employment guide, it will facilitate the teaching of career development by Sociology faculty; increase students' ongoing confidence in their potential; and provide a solid foundation for communicating the transformative power of Sociology to employers and managers in the government, business, and non-profit sectors.

Martha A. Martinez is Associate Professor of Sociology at DePaul University in Chicago, USA. She specializes in Entrepreneurship, Organizations, and Economic Sociology. Her current professional goal is to help sociology undergraduates make a successful transition from school to work and maximize the potential benefits of their Sociology degree in the labor market.

ISBN 978-3-031-41322-3

www.palgrave.com